WALKING THE GR5:
LARCHE
TO NICE

Titles in the Footpaths of Europe Series

WALKING THE GR5:
LARCHE
TO NICE

Translated by Paul Becke and Hugh Fenwick

Robertson McCarta

The publishers thank the following people for their help with this book: Isabelle Daguin, Philippe Lambert, Serge Sineux, Jane Hawksley.

First published in 1990 by

Robertson McCarta Limited
122 King's Cross Road
London WC1X 9DS

in association with

Fédération Française de la Randonnée Pédestre
8 Avenue Marceau
75008 Paris

Managing Editor Folly Marland
Series designed by Prue Bucknall
Production by Grahame Griffiths
Typeset by The Robertson Group, Llandudno
Origination by Toppan Limited
Planning Map by Rodney Paull

Printed in Italy by Grafedit Spa, Bergamo

British Library Cataloguing in Publication Data

Walking the GR5: Larche to Nice.
   1. France. Alps. Recreations. Walking – Visitors' guides
   796.522094448

   ISBN 1-85365-223-7

CONTENTS

Key to IGN Maps

Motorway. dual carriageway	
Major road. four lanes or more	
Main road. two-lane or three-lane, wide	Principal
Main road. two-lane, narrow	
Narrow road. regularly surfaced	
Other narrow road: regularly surfaced: irregularly surfaced	
	Possibly private or controlled access
Field track, forest track, felling track, footpath	
Track of disused road. Road under construction	
Road through embankment, cutting. Tree-lined road or track	
Bank. Hedge, line of trees	
Railway: double track, single track. Electrified line. Station, waiting line. Halt. stop	
Sidings or access lines. Narrow gauge line. Rack railway	
Electricity transmission line. Cable railway. Ski lift	
National boundary with markers	
Boundary and administrative centre of department, district	PF / SP
Boundary and administrative centre of canton, commune	CT / C
	For shooting times, go to town hall or gendarmerie
Boundary of military camp, firing range	x — x — x x —— x
Boundary of State forest, National Park, outer zone of National Park	
Triangulation points	
Church, chapel, shrine. Cross, tomb, religious statue. Cemetery	
Watch tower, fortress. Windmill, wind-pump. Chimney	Tr / Chem.
Storage tank: oil, gas. Blast furnace. Pylon. Quarry	
Cave. Monument, pillar. Castle. Ruins	Mon.
Megalithic monument: dolmen, menhir. Viewpoint. Campsite	P.V.
Market-hall, shed. glasshouse. casemate	
Access to underground workings. Refuge. Ski-jump	Mine / Cave
Population/thousands	183,2 0,4 0,15 0,06
Bridge. Footbridge. Ford. Ferry	
Lake, pool. Area liable to flooding. Marsh	
Source, spring. Well, water-tank. Water-tower, reservoir	Ch. d'Eau
Watercourse lined with trees. Waterfall. Dam. Dyke	
Navigable canal, feeder or irrigator. Lock, machine-operated. Underground channel	
Contour lines. 10 m. interval. Hollow. Small basin. Scree	

| Woodland | Scrub | Orchard. plantation | Vines | Ricefield |

All maps are IGN Orange series. 1:50 000

© I.G.N. – Paris

A note from the publisher

The books in this French Walking Guide series are produced in association and with the help of the Fédération Française de la Randonnée Pédestre (French Ramblers' Association) — generally known as the FFRP.

The FFRP is a federal organisation and is made up of regional, local and many other associations and bodies that form its constituent parts. Individual membership is through these various local organisations. The FFRP therefore acts as an umbrella organisation overseeing the waymarking of footpaths, training and the publishing of the Topoguides, detailed guides to the Grande Randonnée footpaths.

There are at present about 170 Topoguides in print, compiled and written by local members of the FFRP, who are responsible for waymarking the walks — so they are well researched and accurate.

We have translated the main itinerary descriptions, amalgamating and adapting several Topoguides to create new regional guides. We have retained the basic Topoguide structure, indicating length and times of walks, and the Institut Géographique National (official French survey) maps overlaid with the routes.

The information contained in this guide is the latest available at the time of going to print. However, as publishers we are aware that this kind of information is continually changing and we are anxious to enhance and improve the guides as much as possible. We encourage you to send us suggestions, criticisms and those little bits of information you may wish to share with your fellow walkers. Our address is: Robertson McCarta, 122 King's Cross Road, London WC1X 9DS.

We shall be happy to offer a free copy of any one of these books to any reader whose suggestions are subsequently incorporated into a new edition.

It is possible to create a variety of routes by referring to the walks in the contents page and to the planning map (inside the front cover). Transport is listed in the alphabetical index in the back of the book and there is an accommodation guide.

KEY

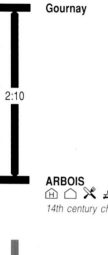

Gournay

This example shows that you can expect the walk from Gournay to Arbois to take 2 hours, 10 minutes.

2:10

ARBOIS

14th century church

Arbois has a variety of facilities, including hotels and buses. Hotel addresses and bus/train connections may be listed in the index at the back of the book.

A grey arrow indicates an alternative route that leaves and returns to the main route.

Detour

indicates a short detour off the route to a town with facilities or to an interesting sight.

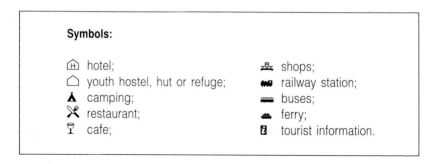

Symbols:

⌂	hotel;	⚒	shops;
⌂	youth hostel, hut or refuge;	⊷	railway station;
▲	camping;	▭	buses;
✕	restaurant;	⚓	ferry;
⅀	cafe;	▤	tourist information.

THE FOOTPATHS OF FRANCE

by Robin Neillands

Why should you go walking in France? Well, walking is fun and as for France, Danton summed up the attractions of that country with one telling phrase: 'Every man has two countries,' he said, 'his own . . . and France.' That is certainly true in my case and I therefore consider it both a pleasure and an honour to write this general introduction to these footpath guides to France. A pleasure because walking in or through France is my favourite pastime, an honour because these excellent English language guides follow in the course set by those Topoguides published in French by the Fédération Française pour la Randonnée Pédestre, which set a benchmark for quality that all footpath guides might follow. Besides, I believe that good things should be shared and walking in France is one of the most pleasant activities I know.

I have been walking in France for over thirty years. I began by rambling — or rather ambling — through the foothills of the Pyrenees, crossing over into Spain past the old Hospice de France, coming back over the Somport Pass in a howling blizzard, which may account for the fact that I totally missed two sets of frontier guards on both occasions. Since then I have walked in many parts of France and even from one end of it to the other, from the Channel to the Camargue, and I hope to go on walking there for many years to come.

The attractions of France are legion, but there is no finer way to see and enjoy them than on foot. France has two coasts, at least three mountain ranges — the Alps, Pyrenees and the Massif Central — an agreeable climate, a great sense of space, good food, fine wines and, believe it or not, a friendly and hospitable people. If you don't believe me, go there on foot and see for yourself. Walking in France will appeal to every kind of walker, from the day rambler to the backpacker, because above all, and in the nicest possible way, the walking in France is well organised, but those Francophiles who already know France well will find it even more pleasurable if they explore their favourite country on foot.

The GR system

The Grande Randonnée (GR) footpath network now consists of more than 40,000 kilometres (25,000 miles) of long-distance footpath, stretching into every part of France, forming a great central sweep around Paris, probing deeply into the Alps, the Pyrenees, and the volcanic cones of the Massif Central. This network, the finest system of footpaths in Europe, is the creation of that marvellously named organisation, *la Fédération Française de Randonnée Pédestre, Comité National des Sentiers de Grande Randonnée,* which I shall abbreviate to FFRP-CNSGR. Founded in 1948, and declaring that, *'un jour de marche, huit jours de santé',* the FFRP-CNSGR has flourished for four decades and put up the now familiar red-and-white waymarks in every corner of the country. Some of these footpaths are classic walks, like the famous GR65, *Le Chemin de St. Jacques,* the ancient Pilgrim Road to Compostela, the TMB, the *Tour du Mont Blanc,* which circles the mountain through France, Switzerland and Italy, or the 600-mile long GR3, the *Sentier de la Loire,* which runs from the Ardèche to the Atlantic, to give three examples from the hundred or so GR trails available. In addition there is an abundance of GR du Pays or regional footpaths, like the *Sentier de la Haute Auvergne,* and the *Sentier Tour des Monts d'Aubrac.* A 'Tour' incidentally, is usually a circular walk.

Many of these regional or provincial GR trails are charted and waymarked in red-and-yellow by local outdoor organisations such as ABRI (Association Bretonne des Relais et Itineraires) for Brittany, or CHAMINA for the Massif Central. The walker in France will soon become familiar with all these footpath networks, national, regional or local, and find them the perfect way into the heart and heartland of France. As a little bonus, the GR networks are expanding all the time, with the detours — or *varientes* — off the main route eventually linking with other GR paths or *varientes* and becoming GR trails in their own right.

Walkers will find the GR trails generally well marked and easy to follow, and they have two advantages over the footpaths commonly encountered in the UK. First, since they are laid out by local people, they are based on intricate local knowledge of the local sights. If there is a fine view, a mighty castle or a pretty village on your footpath route, your footpath through France will surely lead you to it. Secondly, all French footpaths are usually well provided with a wide range of comfortable country accommodation, and you will discover that the local people, even the farmers, are well used to walkers and greet them with a smile, a *'Bonjour'* and a *'bonne route'*.

Terrain and Climate

As a glance at these guides or any Topoguide will indicate, France has a great variety of terrain. France is twice the size of the UK and many natural features are also on a larger scale. There are three main ranges of mountains, the Alps contain the highest mountain in Europe, the Pyrenees go up to 10,000 ft, the Massif Central peaks to over 6000 ft, and there are many similar ranges with hills which overtop our highest British peak, Ben Nevis. On the other hand, the Auvergne and the Jura have marvellous open ridge walking, the Cévennes are steep and rugged, the Ardeche and parts of Provence are hot and wild, the île de France, Normandy, Brittany and much of western France is green and pleasant, not given to extremes. There is walking in France for every kind of walker, but given such a choice the wise walker will consider the complications of terrain and weather before setting out, and go suitably equipped.

France enjoys three types of climate: continental, oceanic, and Mediterranean. South of the Loire it will certainly be hot to very hot from mid-April to late September. Snow can fall on the mountains above 4000 ft from mid-October and last until May, or even lie year-round on the tops and in couloirs; in the high hills an ice-axe is never a frill. I have used one by the Brêche de Roland in the Pyrenees in mid-June.

Wise walkers should study weather maps and forecasts carefully in the week before they leave for France, but can generally expect good weather from May to October, and a wide variety of weather — the severity depending on the terrain — from mid-October to late Spring.

Accommodation

The walker in France can choose from a wide variety of accommodation with the assurance that the walker will always be welcome. This can range from country hotels to wild mountain pitches, but to stay in comfort, many walkers will travel light and overnight in the comfortable hotels of the *Logis de France* network.

Logis de France: The *Logis de France* is a nationwide network of small, family-run country hotels, offering comfortable accommodation and excellent food. *Logis* hotels are graded and can vary from a simple, one-star establishment, with showers and linoleum, to a four- or five-star *logis* with gastronomic menus and deep pile carpets. All offer excellent value for money, and since there are over 5,000 scattered across the French countryside, they provide a good focus for a walking day. An annual guide to the *Logis* is available from the French Government Tourist Office, 178 Piccadilly, London W1V 0AL, Tel (071) 491 7622.

Gîtes d'étape: A *gîte d'étape* is best imagined as an unmanned youth hostel for outdoor folk of all ages. They lie along the footpath networks and are usually signposted or listed in the guides. They can be very comfortable, with bunk beds, showers, a well equipped kitchen, and in some cases they have a warden, a *guardien,* who may offer meals. *Gîtes d'étape* are designed exclusively for walkers, climbers, cyclists, cross country skiers or horse-riders. A typical price (1990) would be Fr.25 for one night. *Gîtes d'étape* should not be confused with a *Gîte de France.* A *gîte* — usually signposted as '*Gîte de France*' — is a country cottage available for a holiday let, though here too, the owner may be more than willing to rent it out as overnight accommodation.

Youth hostels: Curiously enough, there are very few youth hostels in France outside the main towns. A full list of the 200 or so available can be obtained from the Youth Hostel Association (YHA), Trevelyan House, St. Albans, Herts AL1 2DY.

Pensions or cafes: In the absence of an hotel, a *gîte d'étape* or a youth hostel, all is not lost. France has plenty of accommodation and an enquiry at the village cafe or bar will usually produce a room. The cafe/hotel may have rooms or suggest a nearby pension or a *chambre d'hôte*. Prices start at around Fr.50 for a room, rising to say, Fr.120. (1990 estimate).

Chambres d'hôte: A *chambre d'hôte* is a guest room, or, in English terms, a bed-and-breakfast, usually in a private house. Prices range from about Fr.60 a night. *Chambres d'hôte* signs are now proliferating in the small villages of France and especially if you can speak a little French are an excellent way to meet the local people. Prices (1990) are from, say, Fr.70 for a room, not per person.

Abris: Abris, shelters or mountain huts can be found in the mountain regions, where they are often run by the Club Alpin Français, an association for climbers. They range from the comfortable to the primitive, are often crowded and are sometimes reserved for members. Details from the Club Alpin Français, 7 Rue la Boétie, Paris 75008, France.

Camping: French camp sites are graded from one to five star, but are generally very good at every level, although the facilities naturally vary from one cold tap to shops, bars and heated pools. Walkers should not be deterred by the *'Complet'* (Full) sign on the gate or office window: a walker's small tent will usually fit in somewhere. *Camping à la ferme,* or farm camping, is increasingly popular, more primitive — or less regimented — than the official sites, but widely available and perfectly adequate. Wild camping is officially not permitted in National Parks, but unofficially if you are over 1,500m away from a road, one hour's walk from a *gîte* or camp site, and where possible ask permission, you should have no trouble. French country people will always assist the walker to find a pitch.

The law for walkers

The country people of France seem a good deal less concerned about their 'rights' than the average English farmer or landowner. I have never been ordered off land in France or greeted with anything other than friendliness . . . maybe I've been lucky. As a rule, walkers in France are free to roam over all open paths and tracks. No decent walker will leave gates open, trample crops or break down walls, and taking fruit from gardens or orchards is simply stealing. In some parts of France there are local laws about taking chestnuts, mushrooms (and snails), because these are cash crops. Signs like *Réserve de Chasse,* or *Chasse Privé* indicate that the shooting is reserved for the landowner. As a general rule, behave sensibly and you will be tolerated everywhere, even on private land.

The country code
Walkers in France should obey the Code du Randonneur.

● Love and respect nature.
● Avoid unnecessary noise.
● Destroy nothing.
● Do not leave litter.
● Do not pick flowers or plants.
● Do not disturb wildlife.
● Re-close all gates.
● Protect and preserve the habitat.
● No smoking or fires in the forests. (This rule is essential and is actively enforced by foresters and police.)
● Respect and understand the country way of life and the country people.
● Think of others as you think of yourself.

Transport
Transportation to and within France is generally excellent. There are no less than nine Channel ports: Dunkirk, Calais, Boulogne, Dieppe, Le Havre, Caen/Ouistreham, Cherbourg, Saint-Malo and Roscoff, and a surprising number of airports served by direct flights from the UK. Although some of the services are seasonal, it is often possible to fly direct to Toulouse, Poitiers, Nantes, Perpignan, Montpellier, indeed to many provincial cities, as well as Paris and such obvious destinations as Lyon and Nice. Within France the national railway, the SNCF, still retains a nationwide network. Information, tickets and a map can be obtained from the SNCF. France also has a good country bus service and the *gare routière* is often placed just beside the railway station. Be aware though, that many French bus services only operate within the *département,* and they do not generally operate from one provincial city to the next. I cannot encourage people to hitch-hike, which is both illegal and risky, but walkers might consider a taxi for their luggage. Almost every French village has a taxi driver who will happily transport your rucksacks to the next night-stop, fifteen to twenty miles away, for Fr.50 a head or even less.

Money
Walking in France is cheap, but banks are not common in the smaller villages, so carry a certain amount of French money and the rest in traveller's cheques or Eurocheques, which are accepted everywhere.

Clothing and equipment
The amount of clothing and equipment you will need depends on the terrain, the length of the walk, the time of your visit, the accommodation used. Outside the mountain areas it is not necessary to take the full range of camping or backpacking gear. I once

walked across France from the Channel to the Camargue along the Grande Randonneé footpaths in March, April and early May and never needed to use any of the camping gear I carried in my rucksack because I found hotels everywhere, even in quite small villages.

Essential items are:
In summer: light boots, a hat, shorts, suncream, lip salve, mosquito repellent, sunglasses, a sweater, a windproof cagoule, a small first-aid kit, a walking stick.
In winter: a change of clothing, stormproof outer garments, gaiters, hat, lip salve, a companion.
In the mountains at any time: large-scale maps (1:25,000), a compass, an ice-axe. In winter, add a companion and ten-point crampons.
At any time: a phrase book, suitable maps, a dictionary, a sense of humour.

The best guide to what to take lies in the likely weather and the terrain. France tends to be informal, so there is no need to carry a jacket or something smart for the evenings. I swear by Rohan clothing, which is light, smart and functional. The three things I would never go without are light, well-broken-in boots and several pairs of loop-stitched socks, and my walking stick.

Health hazards:
Health hazards are few. France can be hot in summer, so take a full water-bottle and refill at every opportunity. A small first-aid kit is sensible, with plasters and 'mole-skin' for blisters, but since prevention is better than the cure, loop-stitched socks and flexible boots are better. Any French chemist — *a pharmacie* — is obliged to render first-aid treatment for a small fee. These pharmacies can be found in most villages and large towns and are marked by a green cross.
Dogs are both a nuisance and a hazard. All walkers in France should carry a walking stick to fend off aggressive curs. Rabies — *la rage* — is endemic and anyone bitten must seek immediate medical advice. France also possesses two types of viper, which are common in the hill areas of the south. In fairness, although I found my walking stick indispensable, I must add that in thirty years I have never even seen a snake or a rabid dog. In case of real difficulty, dial 17 for the police and the ambulance.

Food and wine
One of the great advantages with walking in France is that you can end the day with a good meal and not gain an ounce. French country cooking is generally excellent and good value for money, with the price of a four-course menu starting at about Fr.45. The ingredients for the mid-day picnic can be purchased from the village shops and these also sell wine. Camping-Gaz cylinders and cartridges are widely available, as is 2-star petrol for stoves. Avoid naked fires.

Preparation
The secret of a good walk lies in making adequate preparations before you set out. It pays to be fit enough to do the daily distance at the start. Much of the necessary information is contained in this guide, but if you need more, look in guidebooks or outdoor magazines, or ask friends.

The French
I cannot close this introduction without saying a few words about the French, not least

because the walker in France is going to meet rather more French people than, say, a motorist will, and may even meet French people who have never met a foreigner before. It does help if the visitor speaks a little French, even if only to say *'bonjour'* and *'Merci'* and *'S'il vous plait'*. The French tend to be formal so it pays to be polite, to say 'hello', to shake hands. I am well aware that relations between France and England have not always been cordial over the last six hundred years or so, but I have never met with hostility of any kind in thirty years of walking through France. Indeed, I have always found that if the visitor is prepared to meet the French halfway, they will come more than halfway to greet him or her in return, and are both friendly and hospitable to the passing stranger.

As a final tip, try smiling. Even in France, or especially in France, a smile and a *'pouvez vous m'aider?'* (Can you help me?) will work wonders. That's my last bit of advice, and all I need do now is wish you *'Bonne Route'* and good walking in France.

THE GR5

by Henri Viaux

President of the French Ramblers Association,1977-1989

The systematic development of long-distance walking in France dates from the immediate post-war period, when two important societies - the Touring Club de France and the Club Alpin Français - began using substantial numbers of volunteers to establish a network of footpaths covering the whole country. These routes became known as 'Sentiers de Grande Randonnée' - 'long-distance footpaths' - soon abbreviated to the simple title of 'GR', each linear or circular route having its own identifying number. The principal aim of the GR paths was to make the best possible use of paths and tracks barred to motorised vehicles, and to reveal rural France in all its richness and variety - the natural wealth of upland and lowland landscapes, the human interest of traditional rural life, and the inherited magnificence of buildings and monuments - combined with enjoyable physical activity. France's mountains have naturally provided an important element of the network. Standardised waymarking was designed to encourage familiarity and confidence in walking: the markings consist of two bars, one red and one white, painted on to any permanent feature along the route.

One of the first footpaths to be planned and established was the GR5, crossing the whole of eastern France from the Luxembourg frontier to the Mediterranean coast on the Côte d'Azur, via the principal mountain massifs - the Vosges, Jura, and the Alps. The route was later extended through Belgium to Ostend.

Completion of the route took a long time, but the most important section, across the Alps - already well-known to climbers, and using traditional tracks familiar to shepherds, itinerant traders, and armies on the march - was soon mapped out and established. The Savoy section of the GR5 was opened to walkers in 1955, extending in due course to Nice and Menton on the Côte d'Azur.

Complementary circular routes were established at the same time in the main mountain massifs, enabling walkers to explore the remote inner mountain areas in greater detail. These too are important GR routes; from north to south, they are: the Tour du Mont-Blanc, across the Vanoise (GR55), the Ecrins - Oisans massif (GR54), the Queyras massif (GR58), the Ubaye massif (GR56), and the Mercantour (GR52).

All these GR routes follow moderate mountain altitudes, between approximately 1,000 and 1,500 metres; any reasonably fit walker can thus explore these great mountain areas without the need for specialised mountaineer equipment. The footpaths lead from col to col and valley to valley, through villages and hamlets where the traditional rural pattern of mountain life still persists almost unchanged: in the mountains it is nature - topography and climate - which commands, and mankind who obeys. Conditions are hard at these high altitudes, demanding endurance and experience and not suited to everyone in primitive huts alongside the flocks in their alpine pastures. For the urban holiday-maker who walks these paths, the encounter with such a way of life can be enlightening and thought-provoking. Nature too has much to reveal to the visitor; summer months bring the delights of flowering alpine meadows, inspiration of the 'mille-fleurs' tapestries. Animal and bird life in the mountains is no less fascinating, for those who are prepared to get up early and go equipped with a good pair of binoculars and plenty of patience: marmots, chamois and ibex can all be seen at various stages along the route, there may be rare birds such as eagles and grouse, the choughs, finches, and many forms of passerines are commonplace. In autumn walkers can enjoy wild raspberries, bilberries, and mushrooms.

Walking the GR5 and its branches demands a sound pair of lungs and good leg muscles; and will specially interest those with a lively curiosity concerning all aspects of nature - though few could walk such a route without being fascinated by its flora and geological structure, and its resident animal life.

Romantic writers of the mid-nineteenth century who discovered the Chamonix Valley, the gateway to the upper Alps, spoke of 'these sublime and terrible mountains'. Human attitudes to the mountains have changed since then, and no-one now would dare to call them terrible; but for the walker who follows the GR5 on a fine summer's day, past majestic rock faces, snow-fields and towering glaciers, the mountains remain truly sublime.

The GR5, North

The northern Alpine section of the GR5 goes through the départements of Haute-Savoie and Savoie, making up the historic province of Savoy which in 1860 voted to become part of France. This is the region of the true Alps, with Mont Blanc their highest peak. The GR5 crosses the area at a relatively modest altitude; starting from Lake Geneva (Lac Léman), the path climbs gently up through the Chablais meadows to the Col d'Anterne, its first high pass. The descent through the Chamonix valley reveals the magnificent ensemble of the Mont Blanc massif; the path curves round to the west of Mont Blanc, southwards to the Vanoise massif and its National Park. Along the way two mountains - from the Tarentaise valley to the Maurienne valley. From the latter the path climbs up to the Vallée Etroite which marks the climatic frontier of the southern Alps.

On its way the GR5 shares its route for some way with the internationally famous Tour du Mont-Blanc GR, which crosses various cols at or above an altitude of 2,500 metres and runs into Italy and Switzerland, with extraordinary views of the great faces and glaciers of the roof of Europe. The route through the Col de Balme to Brévent via the Balcon de la Flégère is one of the most impressive in the whole Alpine massif.

The GR5, South

On leaving Savoy the GR5 goes over the Col de la Vallée Etroite, the climatic threshold of the southern Alps. Here it embarks on a series of mountainous massifs slightly lower than the northern Alps and offering less austere landscapes with the welcoming Névache valley as a typical introductory example. Next the route crosses the Regional

15

Nature Park of the Queyras massif; it is rewarding to turn off at Saint-Véran or Ceillac to walk the GR58 which explores all areas of the National Park.

After crossing the Ubaye massif and the Haute-Tinée, the GR5 enters the National Park of the Mercantour massif in Haute Provence; here it divides in two, one branch leading to Nice and the other to Menton with distant views over the Mediterranean. Here too there is good reason to make a detour, to enjoy the newly established GR of the Mercantour Panorama.

First, however, the GR5 passes the Ecrins National Park, to the left and on a level with Briançon. The Ecrins Park has two important, circular GR routes: the high mountain GR54 path, demanding and occasionally bleak, dominated by impressive rock faces including La Meije; and the GR50, the Tour du Haut-Dauphiné, less strenuous, but offering magnificent glimpses of the high Ecrins peaks.

LARCHE TO NICE

The GR5 follows the Lauzanier valley (Nature Reserve), crossing the impressive Pas de la Cavale to descend to the Tinée, which it follows until Saint-Sauveur-sur-Tinée, passing through Bousieyas, Saint-Etienne-de-Tinée, Auron and Roya. After leaving the Tinée valley it joins the Vesubie valley near Saint-Dalmas-Valdeblore (where the GR52 starts), passing the Brec d'Utelle, Utelle and Levens. Finally it runs parallel to the Var, crossing the hills above Nice and passing through Saint-Claire and Aspremont to reach Nice and the Mediterranean.

The GR52 starts out on the GR5 at Saint-Dalmas-Valdeblore and heads further east. It goes over to Le Boreon by way of the Col de Barn and the Salese valley, then passes the Madone de Fenestre and the Haut-Gordolasque. It then enters the Massif des Merveilles (passing through the valley of Marvels) where there are around a thousand ancient rock carvings. After negotiating the hills of the Menton hinterland (where there is little in the way of accommodation or provisions available), it reaches Sospel, then Castellar and Menton and finally the Mediterranean.

Time of year
By mid-June some of the cols are still thick with snow but often passable. At the end of June and beginning of July conditions are more favourable. The days are long, everything is in bloom and the hotels and refuges quiet. During July and August thunderstorms are common in the afternoons and can be violent. Avoid finding yourself on the ridges at such times.

From 14 July the area is very crowded, slackening off after 15 August. September and early October are much more pleasant. The days are mild but shorter.

The GR5 and the GR52 are practically impassable between 15 October and the end of May, except in the hills close to the Mediterranean, where the altitude is less than 1000 metres (GR5, Utelle to Nice and GR52, Sospel to Menton) and you can get around easily throughout the year.

The mountainous sections of the GR5 and GR52 should only be attempted by experienced mountain walkers, used to walking over varied terrain and carrying a rucksack.

The regions crossed are of two types:
- The mountains between the high pastures and the summits
- The hills of the Côte d'Azur hinterland

As far as the mountains are concerned, remember that, although you are only about 60km from the Côte d'Azur, these mountains are as high as any others in the Alps. Consequently, the walker should not venture into unknown terrain, particularly in bad weather or fog (turn back if necessary). Early in the season, and more so in the Mercantour Massif, the northern slopes of certain cols can present difficulties as a result of snow.

It is not unusual in mid-July to find the Lacs des Merveilles covered with a film of ice in the mornings. On the crossing from Saint-Dalmas-Valdeblore to the Pointe des Trois Communes during the months of July and August, thunderstorms are frequent and very violent after midday. Avoid the ridges during these storms.

The Mercantour National Park

The creation of the National Park in 1979 was a tribute to the extraordinary richness of its flora and fauna, and particularly to the existence of indigenous species, only found in this part of the world (40 plants and nearly 100 insects).

The National Park is in a unique geographical location. It is a high mountain zone which, because of its position in the alpine chain and its proximity to the Mediterranean, is distinguished by:

● Long hours of sunshine typical of the southern Alps

● A landscape of great variety, with cirques, glacial valleys, deep gorges and narrow defiles, cutting up the region into separate areas, each isolated and distinctive Among the flora in the National Park are nearly 2000 of the 4200 species known in France, and about 40 species unique to this area of the Alps. Among these indigenous species the most marvellous is the *saxifraga florulenta*, which has been adopted as the National Park symbol.

All kinds of vegetation are to be found in the National Park: below 700m - Mediterranean vegetation with holm-oak and olives; between 700m and 1,500m - fir, Norway pine and spruce on the shades sides of the mountains; between 1,500m and 2,500m - pitch pine and Siberian pine; above 2,500, - rhododendron, alpine meadows and rocks.

The larger mountain fauna represented are chamois (there are estimated to be around 3,000 in Mercantour); ibex, which come from Italy; wild sheep, which were re-introduced about 20 years ago, and hares of various kinds, but particularly marmots.

The birds are also distinctive: black grouse, ptarmigan, rough legged buzzards and golden eagles.

The insects of Mercantour are more colourful than elsewhere. There are more than 100 indigenous species.

The Mercantour Massif

Some places are particularly wild and rugged, the ultimate setting for Wagnerian epics! Beautiful larch forests cling to the lower slopes. Higher up, these give way to gigantic fallen rocks, and here and there, huge trunks twisted by lightning and wind. Still further up, all vegetation disappears and gives way to enormous rocky planes and cliffs, smoothed and planed down by the powerful action of the great departed glaciers, whose handiwork is perhaps more impressive here than anywhere else. The rock is a schisty crust, covered in many places by a kind of orangey dye produced by the decompostion of iron, and these warm shades contrast with the grey-green rock faces, exposed to the north. All this adds greatly to the beauty and strangeness of the site, which is enlivened by the perpetual movement of the clouds, the murmuring of the water, the whistling of marmots and the clatter of falling rocks disturbed by the chamois.

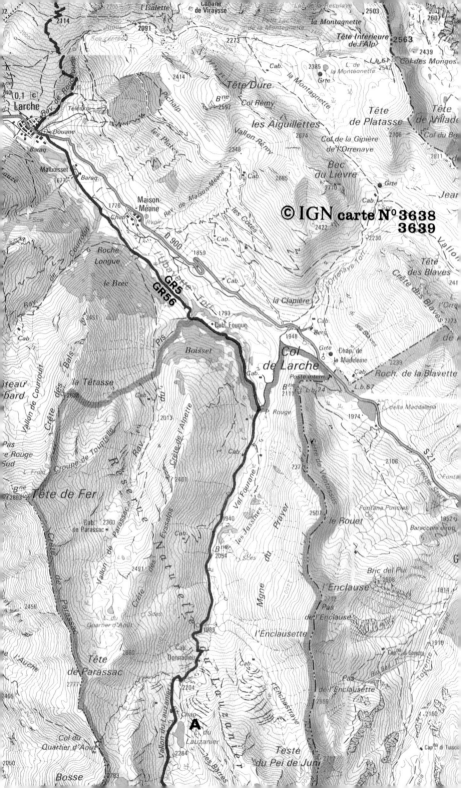

WALK 1

To get to Larche, take the train to Gap (SNCF), then the bus to Barcelonette. Change there and catch a bus (not a daily service) to Larche.

LARCHE

1,675m

Beautiful village rebuilt after destruction by occupying forces in August 1944. Situated at the confluence of the Rouchouze torrent and the Ubayette, and straddling the D900 highway to Italy. Visit the modern church.

1:20

Leave Larche heading south east from the village, along the small asphalt road which follows the right bank of the Ubayette. After the hamlet of Malbois, the road crosses to the left bank of the Ubayette, crossing the Pis torrent (1,787m). Pass the dry-stone Cabane on the left, to reach the approach to Pont Rouge.

Pont Rouge

1,907m

Wooden bridge over the Ubayette. The bridge is at the entrance to the beautiful Vallon de Lauzanier, which you cross. The valley, with the Parassac valley to the west, separated only by the Crête des Eyssalps, forms a nature reserve of 3,000 hectares. It was created in 1935 for the protection of the local wildlife.

1:10

The whole length of the road from Larche takes motor vehicles, but is only gravelled as far as the point where it turns south. It continues to follow the left bank of the Ubayette and climbs the Vallon de Lauzanier. Near the 1,923 metres mark, the Cabane Tardieu (stone-built with sheet metal roof) is on the right; on the left is a pond and another hut. Near the 1,950 metres mark on the right is the Cabane Eyssalps. A little further on, you go past a wooden footbridge over the Ubayette on the left, and cut cross the Lauze Ravine, before arriving at the Cabane Donadieu.

Cabane Donadieu

2,149m

A stone sheep pen with metal roof, occupied in summer.

0:25

The GR5 crosses the Pradon Ravine (at 2,230 metres), passing some ruins on the right. At 2,275 metres, it reaches a new concrete and sheet metal hut, part sheep pen, part refuge, (raised boards for sleeping, table, stove) and the Chapelle du Lauzanier (2,300m). You are now close by the Lac du Lauzanier.

LAC DU LAUZANIER

(See map ref A)

2,284m

A very beautiful location, numerous camping sites and spring water.

1:25

Follow the left bank of the Lac du Lauzanier westward, and continue to climb, passing a rocky spur on the left; cross a stream and follow the east bank until you reach the Lac du Derrière la Croix (2,428m). The road now becomes a track through scree and leads to the Pas de la Cavale.

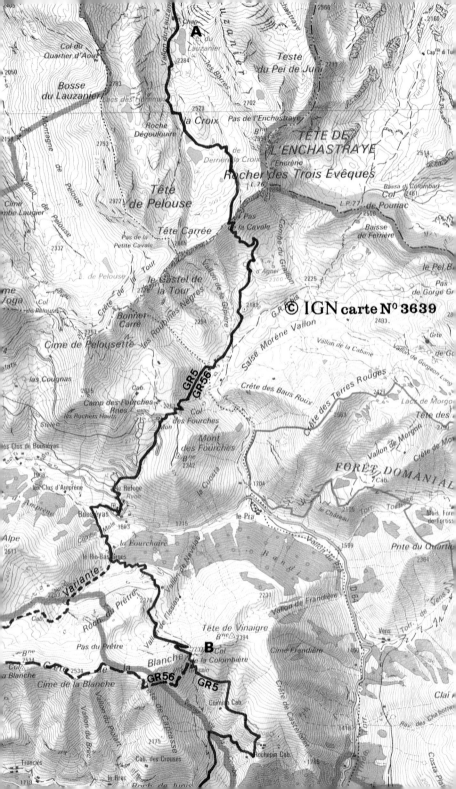

Pas de la Cavale
2,671m

1:25

Lacs d'Agnel
2,343m

0:40

Col des Fourches
2,262m

1:00

BOUZIÉYAS
⌂ ✗
1,883m

1:15

The path winds steeply down the southern slope. Be careful on windy days (the wind is called the *Lombarde*), as stones are blown about and there is some danger of your being hit by them! Over steep, rocky slopes, scree and grass, you finally arrive close by the Lacs d'Agnel.

Pass these small lakes to the east and continue down the left bank of the Gypière Combe. Pass the fork from the Col de Pouriac on the left (approximately 2,095m); 150 metres further on, head east across the Vallon de la Gypière to reach the Salse Morène barns (2,087m).

Bear south west, then west (right) over a track which passes through a dip. Although there are painted stones on the ground, waymarking is infrequent and indistinct. You arrive near a hut. Cross the Tour Ravine and again head south west, then along a diagonally climbing path, to reach Col des Fourches.

On the west side of the col, take the dirt road, then turn to your left to cross the D64, below, near a monument. Go down over the thalweg and cut across a hairpin bend in the road. You reach the road again and follow it right for about 50 metres. Pass round a sheep pen (spring, above it) and leave the road to descend the small Morad Gully. Cross the D64 twice, cut left across another hairpin bend in the road (2,117m), the same again at the next bend and continue down the gully (often dry); you pass an old refuge (1,969m) and on the other side of a mound, you reach the D64 again and Bouziéyas.

Head west from the hamlet along the D64. Go round a hairpin bend, then take a dirt road right, which crosses the Tinée. The road soon turns south east and crosses the Rio stream; a little further on, you cross a large combe. The slope then flattens out; leave the road to take a path. You cut across the road several times, finally rejoining it at Mare Lauzaroutte (shepherd's hut) and follow it until you reach the Col de la Colombiére.

Col de la Colombière
(See map ref B)
2,237m
Junction with GR56 Tour de l'Ubaye
Detour *30 mins*
Tête de Vinaigre
2,394m
Views over the whole of the Tinée Valley

2:00

SAINT-DALMAS-LE-SELVAGE
⌂ ✕ ᠁
1,500m
Very picturesque mountain village at confluence of Sestrière and Valorgues torrents. At the foot of the village, the church, with its Romanesque bell-tower, is worth a visit.

1:00

Col d'Anelle
1,739m
GTA sign

1:10

SAINT-ÉTIENNE-DE-TINÉE
⌂ ✕ ᠁ ⚑ ᠁
1,144m
Popular summer resort beside the Tinée.
Visit the National Park, the 15th century church with its Romanesque bell-tower, and the chapel frescoes.
Keys for the Tinée refuges.

1:45

AURON
⌂ ✕ ᠁ ⓘ ᠁
(See map ref C)
1,602m

Descend to the right bank of the thalweg (meandering course), then cross to the left bank. Do not follow the route on the west side of the ravine (shown on some maps). The path has been washed away in places. The new route shown here passes close by the Cabane Coïmian (in ruins) and the Rochepin barns. Still descending, cross the Vallon de la Combe and following the right edge, you reach Saint-Dalmas-le-Selvage.

Pass on the right of the church, as you leave the village, and continue along a dirt road, twice intersected by the old track, and leading to the Col d'Anelle.

Do not take the footpath south, going down into the valley, but the one going round it on the left (south east). It passes the lower Anelle barns and arrives at West Ublanc, descends steeply to the cluster of Ublanc chalets (Central Ublanc) and arrives at the CD139. Cross the Ardon (1,161m) following the road heading towards the hospital, and you enter Saint-Étienne-de-Tinée.

Go past the gendarmerie, then below the CD39, along a small road which eventually becomes a good path. Past a hairpin bend, you join the D2205 (exD39) near the Chapelle Saint Maur. Head south (left) to take the Auron road (D39) for 200 metres. Leave this by some steps, climbing right, into the forest. You go past an oratory and after a number of tight hairpin bends, arrive at a small col (approximately 1,665m) at the edge of the Auron Plateau. By the 'Chemin de Domandols' (south), you arrive at Auron.

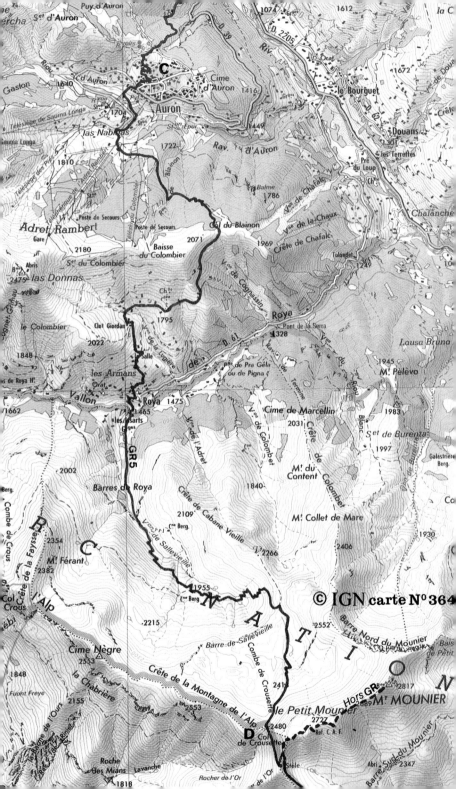

Leading ski resort in the Alpes Maritimes, also a popular summer holiday resort.
Visit the church with its Roman bell-tower and 15th century frescoes.

Detour
Las Donnas cable car

1:30

Detour see left. The Las Donnas cable car (upper station at altitude of 2,256m), operating during the summer, takes walkers up to one of the finest views over the Alps. From the upper station, it is possible to take a short-cut along a track and meet the GR5 at the Col du Blainon.

After Auron Ravine, the GR follows the Riou ski-tow pylons, crosses it and meets one of the Las Donnas cableway pylons. Follow the CD39, and, using the road bridge, cross the Ravine des Nabines (1,652m), pass under the cableway, then by a chalet and a well (the last water point before the outskirts of Roya). Enter the forest, cross the Blainon stream (1,790m) and you arrive at Col du Blainon.

Col du Blainon
2,011m
Connects the Auron and Roya valleys.

1:00

Go down the south slope of the col, past a shepherd's hut (1,922m), then to the ruins of the Chapelle Saint-Sébastien (1,795m); from here, go down into the Vallon de la Lugiére and cross it; after the Salle barns, you come across a wayside cross, then a well and you finally reach Roya.

ROYA
⌂
1,500m
End of the CD61. A mountain hamlet in the wild Vallon de Roya.

3:50

From the hamlet, go down across the Vallon de Roya (1,465m) and into the Mercantour National Park. Then continue along the right edge of the Vallon de la Maïris. Shortly after crossing the Barres de Roya through a gully, cross the Vallon de Sellevieille and continue along its left edge. You arrive at a shepherd's hut (1,966m) in a very desolate location and, along a winding path, you cross alpine pastureland, bearing east beneath the Barre de Sellevieille. Pass by on the left of it. The GR resumes a southerly course, passes over a flat area (springs, and a shepherds' shelter built against the rocky ridge to the west of the GR) and arrives at Col de Crousette.

© IGN carte N° 3640 3641

Col de Crousette
(See map ref D)
2,480m
Between Mont Mounier to the east and Nègre Peak to the west.

At the col, take the road left (south east), which continues the climb up the side of Mont Mounier as far as Stèle Valette (2,587m).

Detour *1hr 15mins*
Mont Mounier
Lookout point.

Detour see left. Following the ridge waymarked with red arrows, in 45 minutes you reach what used to be the Mont Mounier CAF refuge, now in ruins. From the old refuge, an easy 30 minutes' climb takes you to the summit of Mont Mounier (2,817m). There is a lookout point, the first place on the journey from which you can glimpse the Mediterranean and which affords views of the Tinée, Var, Cians, Viso, the Oisans massif and, in clear weather, Corsica.

1:30

Follow the ridge north for about 50 metres, then continue over the east slope. Begin descending, then bear south east. Continue to Baisse du Demant (2,438m) then, skirting the north slope of Mont Demant and passing the Barre du Demant on the left, you quickly lose height and arrive at the Col du Refuge (2,068m). The GR heads east, continues along the north slope of Mont Moulinès and bears north east, before arriving at Col de Moulinès.

Col de Moulinès
1,982m
Detour *1hr 15mins*
BEUIL
🏠 ✕ 🍷 🚡 🚌
1,450m
Head south along a footpath waymarked with yellow arrows (in both directions), following the right bank of the Cians, then take the CD30 for 1 kilometre.

Bear north west, then north east and cross the Demant torrent (1,820m). Following the track (negotiable by motor vehicles) pass by to the left of Pierre du Dimant and cut across the Vallon de Combe Maure. Then, leave the track and follow a scarcely visible path. You pass above the hamlet of Vignols, then cross the Vallon de Gourgette (approx. 1,755m) and climb to Portes de Longon.

1:15

Portes de Longon
1,952m

The GR5 continues eastward along the right bank of the Longon torrent; at the end of the Longon Plateau, it arrives at the large Roure cowshed.

0:20

VACHERIE DE ROURE
⌂

(See map ref E)
1,883m
Converted into a gîte
d'étape. Warden in summer;
catering, water, milk, cheese;
enquire at the Mairie de
Roure 06420 Saint-Sauveur.

1:10

Rougios
1,467m

1:10

ROURE
🏠 ⌂ ✕ 🚂 🚌

(See map ref F)
1,096m
Quaint little village
suspended above the
confluence of the Vionène
and the Tinée. A commune
which has lost more than

1:30

half its population in the past
120 years. See the François
Bréa altar-piece (1560)
depicting the Assumption of
the Virgin Mary and, above

At this point you leave the Mercantour National Park. A little further on the torrent forms waterfalls; the path continues along the left bank in short zig-zags. It crosses the torrent over a footbridge (1,785m) and descends diagonally into the forest, rapidly losing height. You go past the Autcellier ridge (1502m), then the Arcane stream (1463m), into a steep-sided valley, to reach the small overhanging plateau of Rougios.

The GR continues over a region still very alpine, with old wooden alpine chalets, fresh pastures, and larch woods carpeting the ravines.

Enter the Bois de la Frache by the small dirt road which has replaced the footpath; follow it to Roure.

There are views down into the steep-sided Tinée Valley and over the high peaks on the left edge, as well as over the Vallon de Molières plunging eastward. The path continues bearing south east, staying halfway up the wooded slope. You pass the isolated barns of Traverse and Puge de Selvanière, then a small col called *la Barre*. Beyond this, the forest ends and the view opens out onto the Tinée, below. The descent continues southward over the bare slope and you reach some chalets and the Chapelle Saint-Sébastien (frescoes from 1510 A.D. by Andrea de la Cella). Along a small tarmac road, you arrive at Roure.

Junction with the GR52A or Sentier Panoramique du Mercantour which, bearing west, joins the Beuil, Valberg, Haute Vallée du Var; a junction with the Còl de Larche is planned. Eastwards, the GR52A shares the same route with the GR5 as far as Bolline.

The GR leaves Roure (see map ref F) following the old track through numerous hairpin bends and intersects the road several times. You reach the road bridge on the Tinée, which is the gateway to Saint-Sauveur-sur-Tinée.

the high altar, the altar-piece of Saint Laurent and Saint Grat of the same period. Climb to the remains of the château for a beautiful view.

SAINT-SAUVEUR-SUR-TINÉE

🏠 ⌂ ✕ ⚐ ▥ ▭

496m
Largest town in the mid-Tinée Valley, on CD2205. See the 15th century Saint-Sauveur Church and its bell-tower, built in 1333, and the 15th and 17th century paintings inside.

1:40

To leave the town, take the CD2205 south and on the left take the tarmac road climbing to the pretty Chapelle Saint-Roch (approx. 610m). Coming out of the first hairpin bend, leave the tarmac to take a good path on the right. It passes below the chapel, following the old road which used to join Saint-Sauveur with the high villages of the Valdeblore. Cross the Isart ravine (approx. 800m), skirt the Bataille locality, then go round the Roubinastre ravine by a distinctive track cut into steep 'roubines' (Provençal dialect for groups of ravines cutting into one another, like the American 'badlands'). You come out below the village of Rimplas.

Rimplas

1,016m
Built on a steep shoulder surmounted by a large fort and with the Chapelle de la Madeleine standing on a rocky needle. Extensive views over the Tinée and Bramalan Valleys.

1:10

The GR takes the track passing below the road parallel with it and goes into Valdeblore. It joins the CD2565, which it follows downhill for 200 metres, then resumes over the old track on the left, above the hamlet of Planet; you cross the Vallon de Gasc by a small bridge and climb the spur on which the Chapelle de Saint Donnat stands.

Once level with the old glacial terrace, the GR reaches the Church of Saint-Jacques. Here the GR52 turns right, due south, while the GR5 continues straight ahead to arrive at one of the churches of La Bolline - La Roche.

LA BOLLINE - LA ROCHE

🏠 ✕ ▥ ▭

995m
La Bolline, La Roche and Saint-Dalmas form the commune of Valdeblore.

1:00

Cross the CD2565 and continue along the old track which stays below the road and crosses the pastures. Cut across a hairpin bend in the road, pass below the Chapelle Saint-Joseph (1,181m) and you rejoin the road at 1,233m. You follow this road east for 1 kilometre, as far as Saint-Dalmas-Valdeblore.

SAINT-DALMAS-VALDEBLORE

🏠 ⌂ ✕ ▥ ⚐ ▭

(See map ref G)
1,290m

Junction with the GR52 going to or from Menton through the Vallée des Merveilles, and with the GR52A going east towards Saint-Martin-Vésubie (see Walk 2).

Picturesque village on the D2565 where it emerges from Bramafan valley. Popular resort for excursions.
11th century church, built on a crypt dating from the 9th century. The church houses many frescoes from the 14th and 16th centuries.

The GR5 goes south east, continues as far as a reservoir, heads into a forest, skirts a spring and arrives at the Col de Varaire.

1:10

Col de Varaire
1,710m

Without crossing the col, the GR continues first south west along the ridge, then turns right and after a good walk, enters the Noir wood. After a few hairpin bends, you reach Col du Caire Gros.

0:40

Col du Caire Gros
1,906m
Called the Col des Deux Cayres on the 1:25,000 IGN maps. Situated between the Caire Gros to the east and the Caire Petit to the west. Remains of military works, possible shelter in one.

Still climbing in a general south easterly direction, the GR5 continues through alpine pastures, flanking the slope below the skyline. Pass beneath the Tête de Clans and Mont Chalanche to arrive at Le Pertus.

1:00

Le Pertus
1,958m

Continue below the skyline, passing Mount Portissuollo on your left, then pass beneath a power line. Soon after, on the right, there is a bird's eye view of the Chapelle Sainte-Anne, 700 metres below. You reach Baisse de la Combe.

0:15

Baisse de la Combe
1,910m

Pass beneath the Cime de la Combe until you arrive at the skyline. Follow this into the beautiful Manoynas forest. The path, still on the skyline, climbs uphill and towards reference height 1975m where it goes over the north east slope, passing Mont Tournairet on the right.

Mont Tournairet
(See map ref H)
2,086m

The GR passes Mont Tournairet on the right (map ref H) and arrives at Collet des Trous.

0:30

Collet des Trous
1982m

Bear east over a wide path passing over the Cime du Fort. You gradually lose altitude to reach an old strategic road (leading east to the Pointe de Siruol) which the GR takes, although bearing south. You cut off a series of hairpin bends by following a track; you pass a spring

0:40

© IGN carte N° 3741

and, lower down, a chapel, where the route takes a westerly direction along the CD332. It crosses the old military camp of Tournairet (now a holiday camp - the 'Granges de la Brasque') and arrives at a Maison Forestière.

Maison Forestière
1,669m
A spring with plenty of cool water.

0:20

Continue along the CD332, now bitumened, for about 1200 metres to Col d'Andrion.

Col d'Andrion
1,680m

0:45

Leave the road and take a path right, winding down in hairpin bends. You come out onto the road, which you take right for 200 metres; then descend below this road along a good path. You again meet the road on a hairpin bend, then on a second one, follow it for 10 metres to take up the footpath below once again (forestry work has obscured the start of the path on the approaches to the road). The GR continues to descend south and arrives at Col des Fournes.

Col des Fournès
1,356m
Crossroads of several paths.
Beware: *Numerous tree felling sites have created new paths.*

0:45

Heading in a general south south easterly direction, the GR passes along a beautiful route through the forest, and onto the eastern slope. It meets the skyline for the first time and, after passing below Cime de Bellegarde, comes out on the crest again as it leaves the forest at Col de Grateloup.

This is the junction with the *Sentier des Huits Vallées* coming from Tinée (waymarked red and yellow).

Col de Grateloup
1,412m

Still bearing south, the GR passes onto the western slope to cross the ridge (place with the GTA sign indicating the col). Dropping down a little, skirt east past the Casal ridge, and you arrive at the Pras (grassland), where there is a very beautiful view of the Brec d'Utelle face.

Les Pras
(See map ref I)

0:45

At the ruins of Les Pras hamlet (map reference I), pass the *Sentier des Huit Vallées* (waymarked red and yellow) left, and descend towards the Vallée de la Vésubie. The GR5 runs into the forest, remaining at the same altitude. After a climb which follows a line through the rocks, you arrive at La Brèche du Brec.

Col du Brec
1,370m

0:35

Col de la Mei
1,220m
Beneath the curious Castel-

Descend between rocks and then loose stones to Col du Brec.

By a flanking path, collapsed in places, you arrive at Col de la Mei.

The descent continues along a stony path, which passes beneath the Tête de la Pennes, then through old terraced plots. You reach a

0:45

Ginestet rock, which has the appearance of a château-fort, and through which Masséna dragged a cannon in 1793.

UTELLE
🏨 ⌂ ✕ ⚓

821m
Small, once prosperous village, on old mule route from Nice to Tinée. Now a pretty village built on a spur dominating the Vallée de la Vésubie with, as a backdrop, the peaks of the Gordolasque, from which soar Monts Clapier and Capelet, among others. Visit the church of Saint-Véran. An unusual construction, with vaulted 17th century stucco ceilings; beautiful Gothic porch with carved wooden doors, representing the life of Saint-Véran. Inside are: a painting of the Annunciation of the Nice primitive school of the end of the 15th century, a large altar-piece, and a carved wooden high altar and chair of the 16th and 17th centuries.

1:00

Detour *2hrs 20mins by the Madone d'Utelle*

1:00

Sanctuaire de la Madone
A sanctuary of very ancient origin. An orientation chart close by: one of the most splendid panoramas of the Alpes-Maritimes.

0:20

Col d'Ambellard
Sheep pens close by

1:00

Chapelle Saint-Antoine
where you rejoin the GR5.

road, which you cross to enter the village of Utelle.

Walkers wishing to go past the Sanctuaire de la Madone should take the unwaymarked detour, shown on the map by the broken line.

1:00

From the church square in Utelle, head west and descend to cross the Vallon du Rio. Still on a footpath, climb steeply once again, before redescending to cross the Vallon du Cros. The track continues along level ground, passes close to the Olivari barns and arrives at the Chapelle Saint-Antoine.

Chapelle Saint-Antoine
(See map ref J)
676m

From the Chapelle Saint-Antoine (map ref J) the descent continues over a gentle slope down to an altitude of about 600 metres, then becomes more pronounced. Continue to the Colombier wayside cross (403m), then to the chapel of the Cros d'Utelle hamlet (water trough) which dominates the Vésubie gorges. Continue downhill, cutting across the hairpin bends in the CD67 several times; continue to the Madone barns and you join the CD67, which you follow as far as the Carrefour du CD2565.

1:15

CD2565 CROSSROADS
▬
195m
Situated in the locality of the Cros d'Utelle in the heart of the Vésubie gorges.

Cross the road, then the Vésubie over the Pont du Cros and make the stiff climb cutting across the Vésubie canal. Then, through a series of hairpin bends, climb the Fond de Linia Ravine once again and you reach the CD19 (512m). Cut across it and take, on the right, the parallel path overlooking it. You regain the road coming out of the Bonsonnet ravine and arrive at the entrance to Levens.

1:15

LEVENS
🏠 ✕ ⚓ ▬
580m
The GR5 does not cross the village of Levens perched above, but only the part located at the foot of the hill, which is crossed by the CD19.
The Haut-Levens is perched on an eminence in the olive trees, dominating the confluence of the Vésubie and the Var. View deep down over the Vésubie Gorges, the sea, the Nice hills, the snowy peaks of the Argentera, Gelas and Clapier, and the rocky bulks of the Diable and Mount Bégo.

The GR5 continues along the CD19 for 1.2 kilometres (gendarmerie). Take the CD14 right (Saint-Blaise road) for 350 metres up to the north of a large meadow. Turn left on the western edge of this meadow, following a line of pylons set in concrete. Continue along level gound, bearing south east by some old retaining walls. You thus reach a path, still bearing south east, which climbs again to a small hump, before reaching the small (586m) col. You come upon a number of paths: take the first right, slowly descending, then turn left.

This track skirts the Maison André (features on the IGN map), continues over level ground, and rapidly drops to the edge of a valley, descending first the right edge, then the left of it. You come out onto a wide road which you take left to meet the houses of the Bermond hamlet. Then, by some steps, you descend

0:50

© IGN carte N° 37

Curious Gothic church,
decorated with stucco in the
16th and 17th centuries.

SAINTE-CLAIRE

(See map ref K)
500m

onto the road to the village of Sainte-Claire.

Take the road right (south) as far as Lausière
(map ref L). A path climbs a small unnamed
col (565m), and bears south west to a second
hill (609m). After climbing part of the way up

the north east ridge of Mont Cima (an absolutely magnificent view over the whole of the Alpes-Maritimes), skirt the east and south slopes to descend across a small ravine and climb up again onto the opposite edge to reach a road which you follow south. At the top of a rise, leave it for a path left, still bearing south, to join the Collet de la Treille (665m). The path then descends over the west slope (Vallée du Var) down to the Chapelle des Salettes, and a vast car park (and seats). Walk over to the right to find a steep track, at first tarmac then dirt, until you reach the road, which you follow. The road is also waymarked for the 'Balcons de la Côte d'Azur' GR51.

2:15

Detour
The 'Balcons de la Côte d'Azur GR51
Bearing south west, it reaches Colomars and the Vallée du Var; bearing south east, it shares the same route as the GR5 as far as the village of Aspremont.

ASPREMONT
🏠 ✕ 🚎 🚂
500m
Built on a round hillock in concentric alley-ways. Visit the Gothic church and, above the village, the terrace formed by the subfoundation of the old château.

Without entering the village, the GR5 and GR51 follow the D14 road to Nice, passing the D719 on the left (road from Tourrette-Leves). On the right are some steps down to a path. Follow the path to cut across the D14 road.

The GR5 and GR51 continue east south east along a road which they climb to the left bank of a thalweg.

Shortly before the Col d'Aspremont, the GR51 continues straight ahead towards Tourrette-Levens.

The GR5 takes the rapidly climbing path right (south west, then south east). Cross the west shoulder of Mont Chauve d'Aspremont to arrive at an old military road leading right to an old fort (785m, see map ref M).

2:15

Detour *1hr 45mins (there and back)*
Mont-Chauve
853m

Detour see left. When you reach this old military road and take it left, you come out onto a tarmac road leading, left, to the summit of Mont Chauve d'Aspremont (854m), crowned by

41

a fort. A magnificent view over the whole of the Alpes-Maritimes. To the south, the Côte d'Azur and Nice spread out before you, between the hills descending from Mont Chauve towards the sea, the Cap d'Antibes l'Esterel, the countryside of Grasse and the dry limestone plateau of Cheiron (intersected by the GR4). To the north, the frontier range raises its snowy peaks: Argentera, Gélas, Mont Clapier.

The GR5 leaves to the right, the road leading to the D214, and then descends along the western slope of the Graus crest, to arrive by a private tarmac road (Chemin de Châteaurenard) at the Aire-Saint-Michel crossroads.

L'AIRE-SAINT-MICHEL CROSSROADS

ⓗ ▭

314m

0:40 *Sign indicating the GR5*

Take the old Gairault track opposite (placard) terminating at the CD14, turn left and after a hairpin bend, which you cut across by a stairway, rejoin the old Gairault track once again. You arrive at Avenue Henri-Dunant, then Place Alex-Médecin (Saint Maurice quarter), from where no. 1 and 2 buses will take you to the centre of Nice.

NICE

ⓗ ⌂ ⋏ ✕ ⵝ 🚊 🚌
▭ 🛈

Prefecture of the Alpes-Maritimes, 5th largest city in France. Queen of the Côte d'Azur, one of the largest tourist centres in France and Europe.
On the international railway line from Paris to Vintimille, the Provence terminus of the railway line from Digne, and one of the maritime railheads for Corsica. Airport linked by direct flights to a number of cities throughout the world.

Here the GR5, which has set off from Holland to cross Belgium and the whole of France, finally ends its journey.

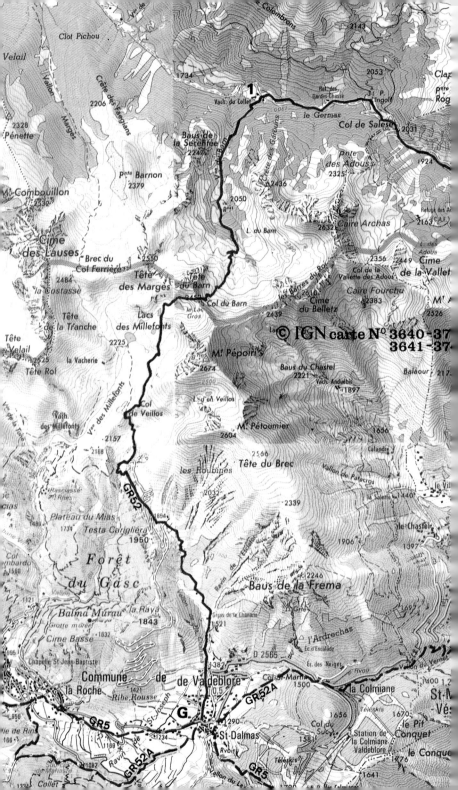

WALK 2

3:00

**SAINT-DALMAS-
VALDEBLORE**
🏠 △ ✕ ⚓ Å ▭
(See map ref G)
1,290m
*On the D2565, where the
Vallon de Bramafan opens
out; a picturesque village
and popular, but quiet,
excursion resort.*
*Visit the 11th century Roman
church, with its crypt dating
from the 9th century. Several
altar-pieces of the 15th and
16th centuries; frescoes of
the 14th century.*

The GR52A leaves the village climbing to the north of the Vallon de Bramafan (or de Chanarie); it passes close to a hairpin bend on the CD2565, then goes on to the Chanarie barns and reaches, after a spell through a forest, a sheep pen at about 1850 metres. Watch out for a small col through which the GR runs.

Since the building of a piste into the high Vallon de Bramafan (or Chanarie) has destroyed the footpath, you have to take the track which passes below the new road. You pass close to a hairpin bend and, higher up, cross the piste to climb to a small col (clearly visible from the sheep pen mentioned above). Then, leave the track and turn into the Vallon de Gasch (Gasc) over a footpath (not featured on IGN maps) which, flanking the mountain, crosses two valleys, then climbs over a grassy brow to rejoin and cross the piste. In this way you reach the old pathway to Col de Veillos.

1:00

Col de Veillos
2,194m
*On the ridge overlooking the
Vallon de Millefonts.*

Leave the track waymarked in blue, which north to Lac Petit (des Millefonts), in fact the largest of these lakes! The GR52 follows the poorly marked track north east, passing Lac Rond and Lac Long on the left, and on the right Lac Gros, to reach Col de Barn.

1:10

Col de Barn
2,452m
*On the ridge between the
Vallon des Molières and Mont
Pépouiri. Boundary of Parc
National du Mercantour.*

An easy descent, at first in the open, still on the left edge of the valley, passing Lac du Barn on your right. You enter a forest and, when you leave it, cross a mountain stream. On the right is the old derelict Vacherie du Collet. The slope becomes easier (nice open spots for camping). When you meet the Vallon de Barn, cross it (1927m), continuing to descend through the forest until you reach Collet dairy farm.

Vacherie du Collet
(See map ref 1)
1,842m
*In the Vallon de Molières.
Water, milk and cheese*

The path, now a dirt road, bears east, climbing the Vallon des Molières some way into the forest. Continue until you reach a clearing (on the left, a hunting hut).The left fork leads up to the Ingolf bridge over the

0:30

1:40

1:10

1:00

available at the dairy farm.

Col de Salèse
2,031m
Connecting the valleys of Molières (Tinée) and Boréon (Vésubie).

BORÉON
1,473m
Small popular summer resort situated in the heart of a pine forest, and at the top of a natural threshold in the valley, where a dam has been built, fed by the Boréon and its tributaries.
Note: *Last place for provisions before Sospel, as the CAF refuges of Madone, Nice and Merveilles offer only a restaurant service, and that only when they have a warden in attendance.*

Pont de Peyrestrèche
(See map ref 2)
1,838m
Wooden bridge over Boréon torrent.

Detour *30mins*
Refuge de la Cougourde
1,935m
Take a footpath heading north. Rejoin the GR52 at the Lac de Trécoulpes. Follow yellow waymarking.

Vallon des Molières, which is a 5 minute walk from the GR52.

The GR52 itself takes the Molières-Boréon road, which crosses a grassland dotted with trees, and arrives at Col de Salèse.

From the col, the GR52 first heads south west along the road, then along the new path laid by the Parc du Mercantour, on the right edge of the Vallon de Salèse.

Near the Terras barns, you rejoin the road and follow it, overlooking the torrent and the Lac du Boréon. A path goes off the GR52 and down to the right, to the lake and hamlet of Boréon.

The GR52 takes the road climbing up to the gîte d'étape, then winds among the chalets. At the end of this road, turn right onto the Col Guilié path (signposted), which you then leave at the first hairpin bend. Bear still further right (west south-west) onto an almost horizontal path, go past the private Refuge du Pelago, climb the right bank of the Boréon (beautiful view of the waterfall) and arrive at the Peyrestrèche bridge.

The GR52 does not cross the bridge, but continues along the right bank of the torrent. Cut across the Vallon de Sangué and cross the Boréon torrent below the Jas de Peyrestrèche (sheep pen).

After crossing the Boréon torrent, the GR5 continues, first heading south, then south east, climbing to the Lac de Trécoulpes.

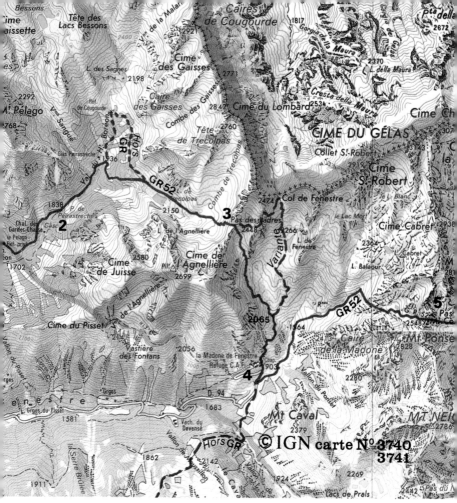

Lac de Trécoulpes
2,150m
GTA sign.

0:50

Pas des Ladres
(See map ref 3)
2,448m
GTA signpost.
Col connecting Madone de Fenestre and Boréon, situated between the west summit of Fenestre to the north and the Agnellière summit to the south west. A beautiful view of the Cirque de Fenestre.

1:00

The path continues to rise, bearing east south-east, at first gently, then through tight hairpin bends (which, at the start of the season, can still be snowed up) to the Pas de Ladre.

From the Pas des Ladres, the GR52 takes the track on the right (south south east) descending below the Cime de l'Agnellière, and you arrive at the junction with the alternative route:

Pas des Ladres
(See map ref 3)
2,448m

0:30

Col de Fenestre
2,474m
Climb up to the highest point
of the col to see the view.
Frontier col with Italy. A very
ancient pass; a Roman road
once went through it.
View right to the Cervin and
Mont-Rose, beyond the
Piémont plain.

0:20

Lac de Fenestre
2,266m

0:30

Junction with the GR52
2,065m
coming directly from Pas des
Landres.

1:00

Madone de Fenestre
(See map ref 4)
1,903m
A small hamlet situated at
the finish of the CD94,
climbing from Saint-Martin-
Vésubie.
CAF refuge with warden.
When this is unattended,
there is a refuge with
accommodation for 20.

1:00

Alternative route from the Pas des Ladres, it is possible to pass through the Col de Fenestre (view over Mont Rose in clear weather) to reach Madone de Fenestre, following a waymarking in the form of three horizontal painted bars (a green bar between two white bars).

Take the path heading east north-east, which climbs up to about 2,250 metres, then drops down again, heading north until just beneath the Col de Fenestre.

Retrace your steps along the path which then descends due south, through numerous hairpin bends. Pass some old military installations and reach Lac de Fenestre.

You walk along the western edge of the lake, before descending to the 'Prairie de Fenestre'. Go past a solitary, black triangular rock at (2,171m) at the Magnin spring, and you arrive at the junction with the GR52.

Due south, the GR52 descends over a track with hairpin bends, to Madone de Fenestre.

Pass by the right of the chapel, go down to the torrent and cross this to climb onto its left bank. Soon, you cut across the Ponset torrent. Cross a grassland dotted with larches and overlooked by Cayre de la Madone. Past the trees, climb the grassland towards a roche moutonnée which is covered with black lichen. Pass by the foot of this rock and you arrive on a spur, from which you can see below the grassland of the Jas Cabret, crossed by several streams. Then climb to the right

Madone de Fenestre

Although a little austere, the location is very beautiful. The hamlet is dominated from north to south by the Gélas (3,143m) and the ridge linking Mont Colomb with Mont Ponset, the ridge which the GR52 crosses at the Mont Colomb pass. In front of Mont Ponset looms the stately Aiguille du Cayre de la Madone. The hamlet is built around the chapel, which has a statue of the Blessed Virgin, attributed by tradition to Saint Luke. Pilgrimages, 27 July, 15 August and 8 September.

You can join the GR52A 'Panoramique du Mercantour' from here by climbing to Baisse de Férisson (1,910m); from there you can reach Saint-Martin-Vésubie, Belvedère or La Bollène.

towards the base of the Cayre de Madone and climb across it in an easterly direction, through heavy scree as far as the Vallon du Mont-Colomb.

0:30

Vallon du Mont-Colomb
2,300m

Climb this valley on its left, first passing over grassy terraces on the right bank of the torrent, which you cross to follow the grassy bottom as far as the Lac du Mont-Colomb.

Lac du Mont-Colomb
2,390m

The lake is dominated to the south by the sugar-loaf summit of Mont Ponset, to the north east by Mont Colomb, and to the east by Cayre-Colomb. It is between this last summit and Mont Ponset that the Pas du Mont-Colomb, which you have to cross, is situated; its narrow gap is already clearly visible.

0:45

Climb this valley on the left, passing over a quite stiff névé, then into scree, where traces of the path are visible; you arrive at the Pas du Colomb.

Pas du Mont-Colomb
(See map ref 5)
2,548m
GTA sign.
Narrow col with a distinctive 'gendarme' rock.

0:40

The descent over the eastern slope (Gordolasque) begins through a narrow gully. The well-marked path twists through numerous hairpin bends, and then gives way to wide scree (south east direction). An easy path leads up the Vallon de la Gordolasque to the spot called La Barme.

La Barme
2,150m
EDF dam which has created an artificial lake in the Fous plain.

0:20

Continue along the lake to go round it by the west, then north banks to reach the Nice refuge, perched on a knoll.

© IGN carte N° 3741

Val des Merveilles
The Val des Merveilles is part of the Parc National du Mercantour; it is a magnificent mountain region, a genuine open museum full of thousands of prehistoric carvings. It should be remembered that these carvings and the surrounding area have been declared Sites of Special Interest and that causing damage to them is punishable by law. Do not walk on the stone floors with hob-nailed shoes or carrying a metal-tipped stick or ice axe.

bank. The GR reaches a third lake (2,294m).

The GR continues bearing south, but along the right bank. It rises appreciably, becomes horizontal, then joins the path from the Pas de l'Arpette, which you do not take. Bear east along the hillside, to reach the Refuge des Merveilles.

REFUGE DES MERVEILLES
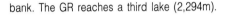
2,111m
Club Alpin Français Refuge.

1:15

From the refuge, following its drainage channel, you reach the Lac Fourcat. Over the east banks, then south of this lake, continue climbing up to the south end of Lac du Trem, then skirt the overflow of the Lac de la Moute (2,274m) on the right. Still climbing (general south west direction) you arrive in sight of the two Lacs du Diable (2,415m) one of which is often dry.

Pas du Diable
(See map ref 7)
2,436m
The GR52 leaves the Vallée des Merveilles.

1:00

Descend south through some hairpin bends, then along a path on the hillside of Serres de Macruère, to arrive at Baisse Cavaline.

Baisse Cavaline
2,107m

0:20

Bear south west, leaving the grass covered knoll of the Cime de Raus on your left, to skirt it to the west, and you arrive at Col de Raus.

Col de Raus
1,999m
This col links Belvédère (Vésubie) and Fontan (Roya).

0:45

Bear south east across the hillside, beneath the Cime du Tuor, which you pass on your right, and you reach the grassy ridge of Ortiguier. Follow it to Baisse de Saint-Véran (1,836m).

Leave the Crête d'Ortiguier, bearing south east and staying on its west flank, until you arrive at the Pointe des Trois Communes.

Pointe des Trois Communes

(See map ref 8)
The main peak of l'Aution, crowned with an old ruined fort, from which there is a splendid view over the whole of the Alpes-Maritimes. Around this fort, several military installations (now put to another use) formerly constituted a strong defensive system, from which, in April 1945, the 1st Division of the Free French Forces dislodged the occupying army after some hard fighting.

Detour *1hr 30mins*
COL DE TURINI
🏠 ⌂ ✕

1,605m

1:00

Water point, the last one before Sospel.

Detour see left. Take the military road on the right, then turn right again onto a short-cut which joins the CD68, a little before the Baisse de Camp d'Argent (approx 1,740m). Follow the road on the right down to Baisse de Turini.

Turn onto the col, situated at the foot of the Pointe des Trois Communes; then descend beneath the ridge (east) to a small col (1,926m). Continue south east over the grass, more or less following the road. Descend, to pass below the old Plan Caval barracks (ruined buildings, danger). Join the CD68 road and follow it bearing south east, then south for about 500 metres, down into a dip (1,859m). Then pass the access road on the right to the dairy farm and descend (south south-west) over the thalweg to the bottom of the Vallon de l'Alp, which you follow downhill over the right bank.

Cross the Vallon de l'Alp on the road, which you then follow for 200 metres to the first hairpin bend; then take the old military road bearing south, passing on your right the Tête de Vaïrcaout (1817m). Leave this road to skirt the east side of Mont Giagiabella (1910m), and after an easy climb you regain the road, which you take south and go past a small unnamed col (1,884m). Take the path on the left above the road and pass beneath the summit of

Maouné (1981m), to arrive at Baisse de Ventabren.

Baisse de Ventabren
1,862m

Skirt the east slope of the Pointe de Maurigon, called Ventabren, along a path. On the right of the track you see a tin shack, then you join the road again to Baisse de la Dea (1,750m).

Cross the Arbouin military road and, bearing south, cross over the west slope (Bévéra) of the Gonella to reach an unnamed col (1706m). From this unnamed col, three paths head south: take the one on the right (Bévéra slope). As this path descends, it skirts the Mangiablo, the last great Aution peak. Still on the west slope, cross a ridge joining the Cime du Ters (west) and the Tête de Gaîs to the east. Continue south as far as Baisse de Linière.

1:45

Baisse de Linière
(See map ref 9)
1,342m

Still heading south, the GR loses altitude, passes the Cime Linière on the right and meets a ridge, then descends south south-east down to Baisse de Fighière.

1:00

Baisse de Fighière
750m
Crossed by a small military road.

Still bearing east south-east, go over the terraced plots; you soon find yourself above the military road, which you then take for about 400 metres; then bear south over terraced plots to Sospel.

1:15

SOSPEL

350m
Pleasant little summer holiday resort, an ancient medieval free town, in a pretty location - in a green basin of terraced plots surrounded by stark mountains.
Junction with the GR52A 'Panoramique du Mercantour'.

Leave Sospel by the CD2566 (Menton road). At the first hairpin bend, leave the road and continue along the path on the left, which climbs to a valley on the right edge of the Plan Germain. Go down into the Roulabre stream and climb up again onto its right bank. Go round to the north of a mound and climb up again to cross the Vallon des Agreux and reach Col Razet.

2:15

Col Razet
1,027m
Five track intersection.

Continue almost horizontally under Mont Abo, bearing south east. You reach a small marsh (1,060m). Take water from the springs and not from the stream below. You are at the foot of Col de Treitore.

0:20

© IGN carte N° 37

Col de Treitore
Situated on the Franco-Italian frontier. View of Italy.

1:00

Prairie de Morga
810m
Detour *1hr*
CASTELLAR
390m
Take the Col Saint-Bernard path bearing west, from which you descend along a good track to Castellar.

1:00

Col du Berceau
1,090m
Situated between the Restaud peak to the east and the Roc d'Ormee to the west.

0:30

Plan de Lion
(See map ref 11)
716m
ESSI sign at the junction with the Sentier des Balcons de la Côte d'Azur, GR51, which you can take west to reach Castellar 1 hour away.

1:30

From the small marsh bear south, skirting the west slope of the frontier ridge. Go on to the Col Basse (1,105m), passing the Grand Mont on your left, then continue to Baisse de Fascia Fonda (965m). The track, still descending south, runs along the right bank, goes through numerous hairpin bends and reaches the bottom of the valley. Eventually you pass close to a large house situated to the north of Prairie de Morga.

The GR52 still continues bearing south over level ground and crosses the Prairie de Morga, where in past times there were many cultivated plots, as the retaining walls indicate. You reach a track taking vehicles, which you climb up to the second hairpin bend; where you leave it and take a path leading to Col du Berceau.

From the Col du Berceau, the path goes through a hairpin bend and descends into the Combe de Berceau as far as a junction of tracks called the Plan de Lion.

The GR52 continues south, gently climbs to the first small col, climbs further, passing a spring and reaches a second small col (748m) with sign-posts. Leave the GR52 and descend towards Italy (east). The GR52 takes a path, at first diagonal, then going through a series of hairpin bends. You see views over Menton, Le Cap Martin, Monaco and the sea, and after rapidly losing altitude, cross a small ridge. Then cross the track from Castellar to Baisse de Saint-Paul (sign-posts).

Continue due south over a good path on the centre line of the slope; you cross a dirt road and a little lower down arrive at a tarmac road, and take it to another road leading under the motorway. Next, cross a small hill and take a track, marked 'Private', due south; a few metres further on, leave this to take a good path descending left. You come out at Rond-Point des Colombières.

© IGN carte N° 3742

Rond-Point des Colombières
110m

0:30

MENTON
🏠 ⌂ ✕ ⚒ ⛺ 🚻

A pleasant summer and winter resort near the Italian frontier.
See old Menton, the Church of Saint-Michel, in front of which in the month of August is held the International Festival of Chamber Music, and the market by the port. Further away, the Monastère de l'Annonciade and the villages of Sainte-Agnès and Gorbio are also worth a visit.

The GR52 takes the tarmac Colombières track for 300 metres and, coming out of the bend, goes down a lane on the right with large stairs. Cross the Boulevard de Garava, continue to descend the lane stairway and reach a road to the north of the railway. Pass below the railway, turn right to reach Menton station.

Continuing south, along the Voie Porte de France (sea front), you will find on your right the bus-stop for buses heading west to the centre of Menton.

WALK 3

The GR6 leads from Haute Ubaye to the alpine foothills of Digne, an area where hard limestone (Clues de Barles, Sisteron) alternates with black marl and rounded sandstone formations.

From high grasslands and larches, the route leads down to a Mediterranean countryside of thyme and lavender, almond and olive; from the land of the 'Mexicans' of Barcelonnette to that of the Provençale storytellers, Giona and Maria Borelly, Marie Mauron and Marcel Scipion.

As it descends the upper Ubaye, the GR6/56 skirts the impressive forts of Tournoux, passes below the ski runs of the resort of Sainte-Anne and then follows a level track above Riou Bourdoux before meeting the structure that geologists call the 'window' of Barcelonnette. Footpaths lead down from here to Barcelonnette itself. At Revel-Méolans, the path continues along the left bank of the Ubaye, reaching the Abbaye de Lavercq via the Col de Séolanes.

The GR6 now climbs the Blanche de Lavercq and follows the ridges to reach the passes of Allos, Cayolle, Restefond and Larche. From here, the path passes by the foot of the Fort de Virayssse and returns to its starting point at Saint-Paul-sur-Ubaye.

From Lavercq, the GR6 heads west until it reaches the glaciated plain of Seyne-les-Alpes, once a supplier of mules to the army but now a resort for tourists in both summer and winter. Near the ski station of Chabanon, the path leaves the plain. Now, with altitudes generally less than 2,000m, the vegetation becomes more Mediterranean and, though the peaks may be less striking, they have their own charm. The route now passes to the north of the famous Clues de Barles, cross valleys which are best seen in autumn. After reaching the forest of Fontbelle, it then passes through the forest of Vanon, following the south side of the Saint-Geniez road and of the Defilé de la Pierre Écrite (D3).

Villages, partly derelict, now become more numerous. From D'Entrepierres to Sisteron, the path runs along the southern flank of the Montagne de la Baume until it reaches Sisteron, where the wide, green waters of the Durance seem more like lakes than rivers. On the right bank of the Durance, the GR6, now sharing the route with the GR946, continues west towards Les Baronnies or Le Ventoux.

CLAUDE BRAUN

The GR6 really starts at Fouillouze, where it meets the GR5 coming from Queyras - a long way from its start in Holland!

Fouillouze is a walk of 1 hour and 30 minutes from Saint-Paul-sur-Ubaye and there is overnight accommodation there (see the guide at the back of the book).

The GR56 (the Tour de l'Ubaye) also passes through Fouillouze, the route here being described counter-clockwise. It shares the route with the GR6 as far as the Abbaye de Lavercq.

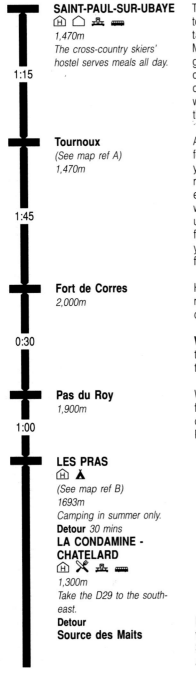

SAINT-PAUL-SUR-UBAYE

1,470m

The cross-country skiers' hostel serves meals all day.

Tournoux

(See map ref A)

1,470m

Fort de Corres

2,000m

Pas du Roy

1,900m

LES PRAS

(See map ref B)

1693m

Camping in summer only.

Detour *30 mins*

LA CONDAMINE - CHATELARD

1,300m

Take the D29 to the south-east.

Detour

Source des Maits

The red and white waymarkers of the GR6 are to be found at the Mairie. Facing the Mairie, take the footpath going down to the Riou-Mounal which you cross by a footbridge. With grassland on either side, continue until you come to the Vars road. Cross the road, and climb the steep slope which leads up to a wide track. Follow the left or southern side of the track to the village of Tournoux.

As you come into the village (drinking fountain), take the road going down in front of you. As you leave, follow the footpath on the right which passes through some fields before entering the forest. Continue along the path, which cuts across forestry and military roads, until you come to the first fort. The GR now follows a wide, well-defined path which takes you up the side of La Condamine to a second fort, called the Fort de Corres.

Here, the GR turns right along the mountainside on the old track, leading to Pas du Roy.

Warning Though safety measures have been taken, this stretch is very tricky and you should take care.

Walk down to the stream and cross by the footbridge, continuing straight ahead across country until you come to the hamlet of Les Pras.

Detour see left. Here, there is also a route without waymarkers, linking the GR6 to the Source des Maits (via the resort of Sainte-Anne-la-Condamine - 30 minutes' walk from

Les Pras - where there are hotels and restaurants). The final stretch is along the 'Chemin Horizontal', a vertiginous path which should only be attempted by the sure-footed. Along the way, it is possible to go down to Jausiers.

1:30

JAUSIERS

This detour is indicated by a dotted line on the map.

From the hamlet of Les Pras , the GR6 climbs the forestry road to the Cabane du Grand-Parpaillon.

Cabane du Grand-Parpaillon
2,031m

Leave the road, which zig-zags up the mountain, and head off southwards along the floor of the deep and almost level valley, the track passing a burnt out fortification on the way. At the end of the valley, the track follows the left bank before coming to an area of small lakes and eventually the Col de la Pare.

2:30

Col de la Pare
2,655m

From the Col de la Pare, the GR6 goes down the Barcelonnette side to the Source des Maits.

0:30

Source des Maits
(See map ref C)
2,284m
Detour *2 hrs 30 mins*
BARCELONNETTE

1,140m
Take the marked detour which goes down in a generally southerly direction.

This point is a junction for the unmarked route from the hamlet of Les Pras and for the marked detour down to Barcelonnette.

The GR6 crosses the 'Chemin Horizontal' and then turns right onto a footpath, leading west to the Maison Forestière de la Pare.

1:00

MAISON FORESTIERE DE LA PARE

1,832m

The GR follows the road down to Barcelonnette. After about 1 kilometre, take the road which rises in a south-westerly direction towards a new hut. At the first hairpin bend, turn left on the road which runs gently down to the Chalets de Chanenponse.

1:00

Chalets de Chanenponse
1,813m

Where the country road bends left, take the slightly rising footpath, which starts from behind the sheepfold, and follow it above an area of felled trees until it reaches the crest of the grassy ridge separating the Barcelonnette from the Thuiles side. Go down the ridge until you reach a sheepfold (1,834m) and then take the Les Grimaudes country road, following it west until you come to the end. A footpath

© IGN carte N° 3538 3539

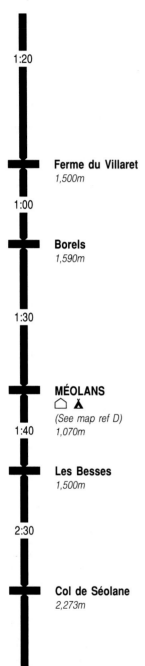

1:20

Ferme du Villaret
1,500m

1:00

Borels
1,590m

1:30

MÉOLANS
⌂ Ⱥ
(See map ref D)
1,070m

1:40

Les Besses
1,500m

2:30

Col de Séolane
2,273m

then continues on the level till you come to a ridge which has been cleared of trees. Cross the ridge and take the track down. When you come out of the wooded area, turn right and then left. About 200 metres further on, turn right onto a track which leads north between properties. Cross the Torrent des Thuiles (very unstable ground for 50 metres). Once on the country road, follow it down as far as the left-hand bend overlooking the old Ferme du Villaret.

On the right-hand side of the bend, look for a track going up into the Forêt des Pinarées. After crossing the Torrent de Champfert, follow the path which leads down between properties to Borels.

Now, follow the stream above the village in a westerly direction. Pass by the houses of Donadieux on your right and take the track down to Rioclar Bas via La Teissonnière before continuing on to Les Reyniers. Take the track which follows the left bank of the Torrent de l'Abéous until you get to La Fresquières. Continue westwards along the road for 500 metres and then cross the bridge over the Ubaye into Méolans.

Go south through the village and then take the tarmac road towards Gaudeissard. As you enter the hamlet, turn left onto the dirt road which will bring you to Les Besses, ignoring the forest track to Montourioux on your left.

300 metres beyond the village, after the water tower, turn left onto the footpath which leads upwards into the forest. (Don't follow the jeep track which continues straight ahead.) The path disappears in grassy woodland at an altitude of 1,750m. The GR crosses a small stream and, clearly marked, climbs through mountain pasture to the Col de Séolane.

The GR leaves the Col de Séolane, turning west to get round a barrier of rock. Reaching a ridge, it winds south until you come to a good, level path on the right (west north-west). 500 metres further, turn left onto a footpath, which takes a long hairpin to bring you to a grassy slope.

1:15

The route passes close to a barn and then the path joins a well-marked track, descending towards Le Duc. However, before reaching the old hamlet, the GR turns left (south east) towards the Les Sartres chalets.

Now, turn left on the gravelled road and cross the Torrent du Bachas at the first bridge. Before reaching the next bridge, the GR turns off to the left at a bend and follows a path down to the Abbaye de Lavercq.

ABBAYE DE LAVERCQ
⌂
(See map ref E)
1,600m
An old priory attached to the Abbey of Boscodon near Embrun.

At this point, the GR6 and the GR56 go their separate ways.

The GR56 (the Tour de l'Ubaye) now continues along the jeep track, leading south east towards the end of the valley.

The GR6, on the other hand, takes the gravelled road to the west, soon merging into a tarmac road which runs alongside the Torrent la Blanche. The road passes above the hamlet of Clarionds and then a sawmill. It crosses one wooden bridge and then another. About 50 metres further on, turn left onto a footpath which links up with the road to the hamlet of Saint-Barthélémy. Follow this left for 30 metres and then turn left onto a grassy lane which brings you up to the hamlet within a few minutes.

4:30

The GR6 leaves Saint-Barthélémy along a footpath which rises north north-west up the hillside. After climbing for about 10 minutes, turn left and go south south-west along a well-defined track. This soon brings you to a spring, which - it is worth noting in hot weather - is the last place to obtain water before the col. The GR6 continues to follow the hillside on a gentle slope, giving views over the valley below. At the Charence ravine, it reaches an altitude of 1,700m. Here, you cross the thalweg and zig-zag upwards through a forest of larches. You cross a clearing and continue along the mountainside before emerging into meadows and passing a little below a shepherd's hut. Now, the way takes you uphill to the south west in a wide corridor between two peaks until you come to the alpine meadows of the

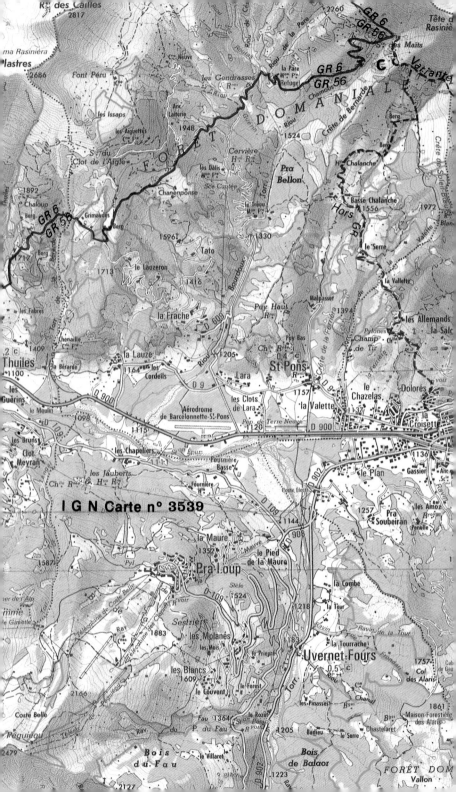

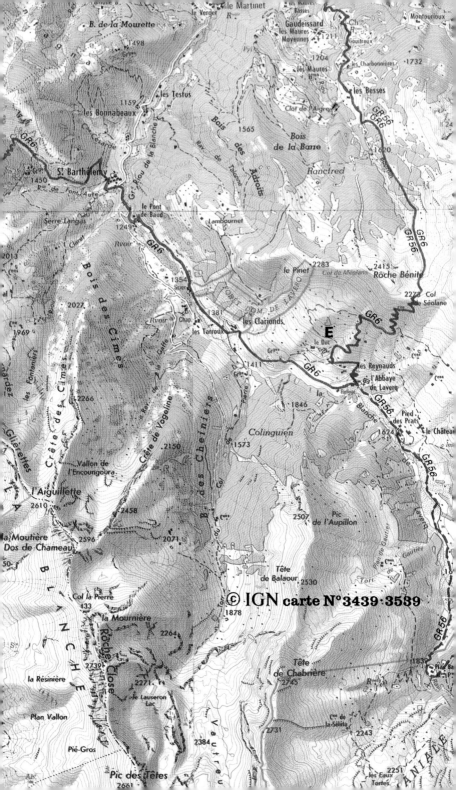

© IGN carte N°3439·3589

Col de Bernardez
2,304m
Panoramic view of the Seyne valley.

2:45

Maison Forestière de Bellevue

About 50 metres to the right, there is a picnic area.
Many species of conifer are to be seen: fir, black Austrian pine, larch and cedar.

SEYNE
(See map ref F)
1,262m
Main town of the Vallée de la Blanche; dominated by the ruins of a Vauban fort and a medieval tower. Fine 12th century church, very similar, if on a smaller scale, to Notre-Dame-du-Bourg at Digne. Also worth seeing are the remains of the fortifications, Porte de

1:15

Provence, the square towers and Chapelle des Dominicains with its triangular bell-tower. The valley, which was not accessible by road until 1825, was inhabited by Ligurians and Gauls as far back as the 6th century BC. It has seen invasions and religious wars and was a Protestant stronghold before being pacified in the reign of Henri IV.

Col de Bernardez, which is clearly visible because of its cross.

The way down from the col is easy, following a small footpath along the side of the mountain. Branch off towards the source of the Chandelette. The GR continues downwards through a state forest and meets a tarmac road about 20 metres before the Maison Forestière de Bellevue.

At this crossroads, you will find the red and yellow waymarkers of a departmental footpath, linking Lac de Serre-Ponçon to Lac de Castillon, a route that takes 7 or 8 days.

The GR now runs south along a foothpath to the village of Saint-Pons. Go through the village and then along the D607 for 1.5 kilometres before taking the old road leading into the small town of Seyne.

The GR leaves Seyne by a tarmac road leading to Bas Chardavon. When you come to the chapel, leave the road and follow a pleasant track north north-west to the Carrefour de la Route de Selonnet.

Carrefour de la Route de Selonnet
(See map ref G)
Shortly before the crossroads, there is camping available at a farm.

1:40

Turn right to get to Selonnet (refreshments).
Turn left for an overnight stop at Surville.

The GR crosses the Selonnet road and you continue through the hamlet of Surville before climbing a stony track towards the alpine meadows of Chauvet. After about 1 hour and 10 minutes, turn off right along the forestry road till you come to the sheepfold at La Montagnette.

La Montagnette
(See map ref H)
1,591m

From here, there are two ways for the walker to get to the Col de Clapouse:
1. A route via Bayons which is 3 hours away (overnight stop).
2. A route via the ridges of the Montagne de Val-Haut. Allow 6 hours and 30 minutes to reach the Refuge du Seignas (no warden) at the Col de Clapouse.
The two routes join at the Col de Clapouse.

Route via Bayons
Remember that the walk from Bayons to the Col de Clapouse takes about 7 hours.

At La Montagnette (1,591m), leave the track which leads south and then south west towards the ridges of the Montagne de Val-Haut. The GR continues west and then north north-west along the forestry road. After about 15 minutes, the GR turns sharply left and then follows the side of La Montagnette. Some gullied stretches now have to be negotiated before you enter the forest and reach the Refuge Forestier.

Refuge Forestier
1,338m
The refuge belongs to the ONF (the National Organisation of Foresters). Part is open throughout the year but there is no warden.

From the ONF refuge, follow the forestry track north west for 150 metres and, where it forks off to the north, continue along the track which winds its way over the side of the Long Coulet.

After a few bends, you emerge into a meadow (1,093m). As this is private property, please be sure to close gates carefully.

3:00

The GR continues along the forestry road beside the Torrent de la Sasse until it reaches a bridge (1,009m). On the other side, leave the main forestry road and take the path on the left bank of the torrent towards Chabanette (derelict farm). At a bend, take the wide

© IGN carte N°3439

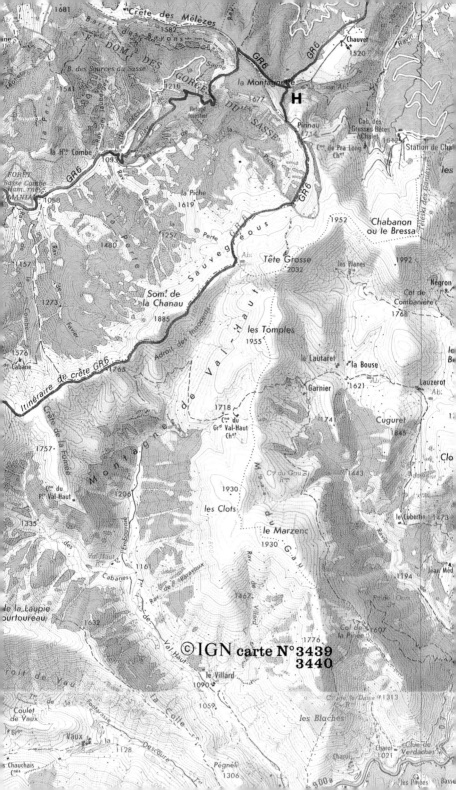

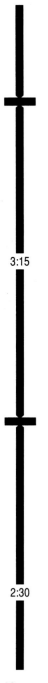

footpath and zig-zag your way across red marl gullies down to a marshy area (900m) which has to be crossed before you rejoin the main forestry road. Follow the road south west until you come to the D1 road which continues in the same direction to the village of Bayons.

BAYONS
⌂ ♨ 🛈
(See map ref I)
875m

Coming into the village of Bayons, the GR crosses the Pont du Sasse. Pass the tarmac road on the left and turn directly south on the forestry track. After a steep rise, you come to a pleasant footpath which zig-zags gently up through the forest. You come out onto a wooded ridge which is crossed by a barely marked pass at an altitude of 1,542m.

Follow a track which leads south south-west and then along the edge of a terrace of pines before dropping down to the floor of the ravine. Here, the track is level until the downhill stretch into Esparron, which begins as a well-marked footpath and then continues as a series of short zig-zags.

3:15

When you come out of the pine wood, cross the Ravin de la Favière and then a small gullied stretch. Follow a lane between dry-stone walls, ignoring a track to the left, and continue until you come to the hamlet of Pont. Now, take the tarmac road to the village Esparron-la-Bâtie.

Esparron-la-Bâtie
1,220m

In the village, take the road which goes up through an area cleared of trees and eventually enters a plantation of pines.

When you come to a fork, take the wide path to the right which rises to the Crête de la Pine (1,428m).

You now pass under the Rocher de Cournaud and then follow the line of the ridge. This brings you to an ONF shelter, part of which is open throughout the year.

2:30

Skirt the northern edge of a lake and then take the forestry track in a south easterly direction. The track bends north but then returns again towards the south east. At an altitude of 1,428m, leave the path for a well-marked track through a beech wood and out into the pastures of La Clapouse. (This is private property: dogs must be kept on a leash and their owners will be liable for any damage caused to flocks.)

Continue uphill through the pastures until you reach the Col de Clapouse.

Col de Clapouse
(See map ref J)
1,692m
The pass is marked by a cairn.

Junction with the route coming from the ridges of the Montagne de Val-Haut.

From the col, it takes 15 minutes to reach the Refuge du Deignas, which is open throughout the year but has no warden. Spring water.

Route via the ridges of the Montagne de Val-haut

From La Montagnette (1,591m), ignore the forest road, which heads west, and, instead, follow the track which turns first south west and then south towards the ridges. You emerge into a vast natural amphitheatre overlooking the valley of the Sasse. The barely marked path crosses shale slopes which are gullied and very steep. The way passes below the summit of Tête Grosse and then joins the ridge of Val-Haut (1 hour 30 minutes). The GR now follows the ridge for about 4 hours, passing by the summits of L'Oratoire (2,071m - fine panoramic view), Clot Ginoux and La Laupie. You then walk down to the Col de Clapouse.

6:30

Col de Clapouse
(See map ref J)
1,692m

From the Col de Clapouse, continue northwards, climbing along the crest of a pasture, with the Vieille Cabane de Chine visible to the west and the Cabane de Clapouse to the east. Following the mountainside, you will reach the Col de la Croix de Veyre.

1:00

Col de la Croix de Veyre
1,886m

The path starts by following the left bank of the Vanon down the southern slope, through meadows in which, depending on the season, you will find primrose, wild tulip and edelweiss. You then come to a shelf, which is often waterlogged. With a pine plantation to the right of the stream, you continue down the left bank through scree and across pastureland where it is easy to lose the path among the many sheep tracks.

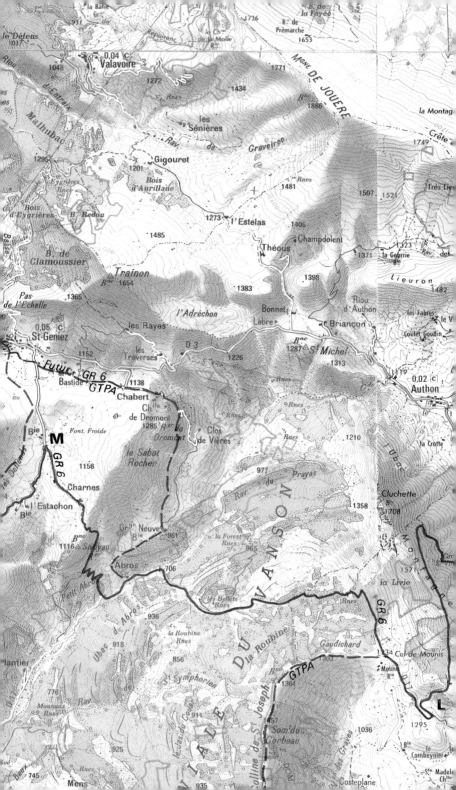

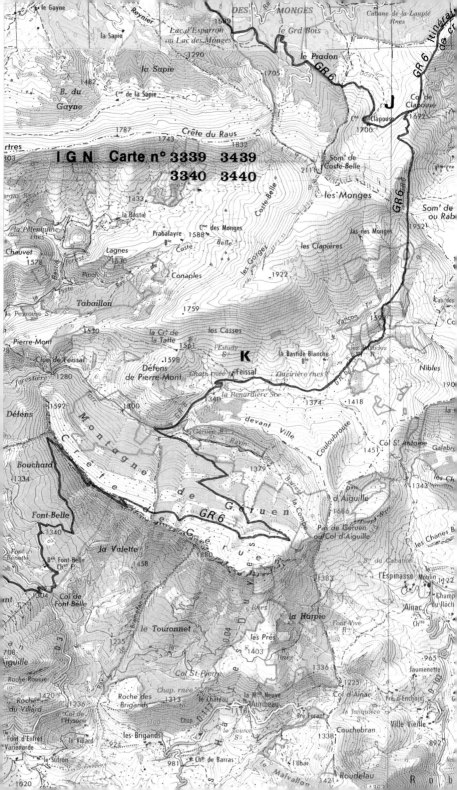

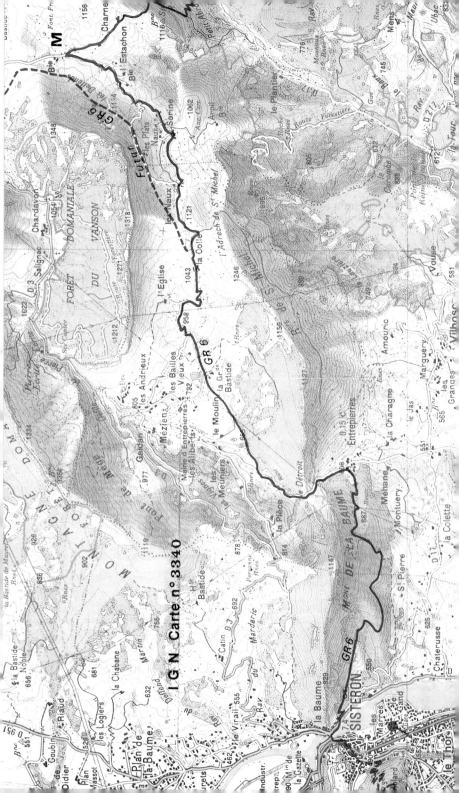

pass in front of the La Colle farm (1,043m). This brings you to the Route de Mézien.

Route de Mézien
712m
A very beautiful church.

0:45

Turn left off the road onto a track alongside a field. Cut across to the right through the grass (no path). After you cross a brook, the path starts again on the left and runs down to the farm of La Grande Bastide. Beyond the buildings, you come to a road. Turn right and proceed for 20 metres before turning off to the left on a path which runs downhill. When you get to a farm, branch left. 100 metres after a little bridge, cross to the other bank of the Caille next to a telegraph pole and take the path to the left. The GR passes through a beautiful narrow gorge between the Montagne de la Beaume and the crags of Saint-Michel. The path hugs the side of the Montagne de la Beaume as far as Entrepierres.

Entrepierres
608m
The village is being restored.
Spring.

3:00

Enter the village through a porched gateway (drinking water fountain on a footpath to the left). Leave by a path which rises towards the Montagne de la Beaume. From here to Sisteron, the GR passes through woods of oak and pine and moorland with broom, box, thyme and lavender. After a steep rise, the GR passes through some small sandpits, turns down and comes to a difficult path (from which it is possible to climb up to the Trou d'Argent over a scree slope). Because of the difficulty, the GR passes by this path on the right and drops down to the D17 road which then leads to Sisteron.

Sisteron
500m
This picturesque town stands on one of the transverse valleys of the Durance, forming an imposing gateway between the Dauphiné and Provence.
Church of Notre-Dame, old Romanesque cathedral; remains of the 14th century battlements; massive 16th century fortifications built by a precursor of Vauban.

The GR6 continues west from here towards Beaucaire.

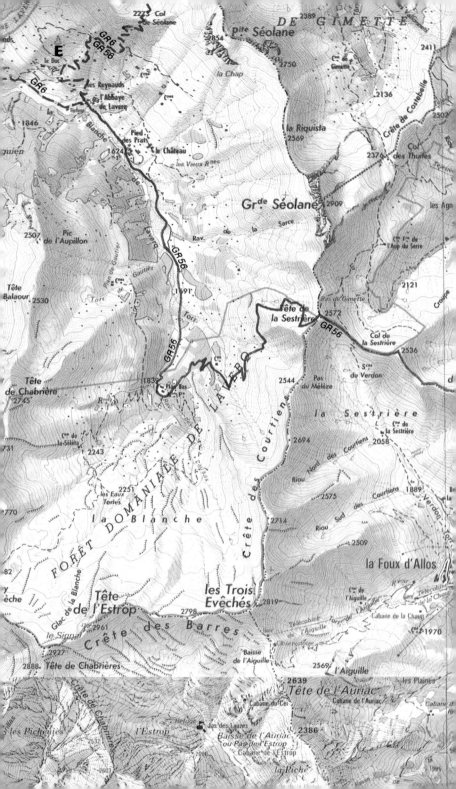

TOUR DE l'UBAYE

The Tour de l'Ubaye (GR56) which starts and ends at Saint-Paul sur Ubaye, follows the same route on the GR6 as far as the Abbaye de Lavercq, already described at the beginning of Walk 3.

The Tour de l'Ubaye (GR56) uses the GR6 as far as Lavercq.

ABBAYE DE LAVERCQ
⌂
(See map ref E)
1,600m

1:15

Whereas the GR6 follows the gravelled road to the west, the GR56 takes the jeep track which rises south south-east towards the end of the valley. At the hamlet of Pied des Prats, the track becomes a foothpath, rising gently up through the forest until it comes out at the Clairière de Plan Bas.

Clairière de Plan Bas
1,839m
Forestry house and
shepherd's hut.

0:45

The GR leaves the Clairière de Plan Bas by a good footpath which, after cutting through undergrowth for 200 metres, turns north north-east. After passing a rock-step, the path zig-zags upwards through woods until it reaches a marker.

2,050 marker
The marker is situated close
to a hut where the GR leaves
the forest and moves into
alpine pastures.

2:40

Follow the pastures first south east and then north east, crossing several gullies. After one last hairpin, the path reaches the Tête de la Sestrière.

Tête de la Sestrière
2,572m
This is the point of
separation between the
waters of the basin of
Lavercq and that of La Foux
d'Allos.

2:00

The GR56 follows the ridge to the south east, passing by the Tête de Vescal (2,516m) and descending to the Col d'Allos.

COL D'ALLOS
⌂
(See map ref 1)
2,240m
Accommodation has warden
in summer, closed in winter.

From the refuge, go south along the road for 100 metres before turning left onto a path with a barrier at the entry. This takes you through an area of springs until you reach La Baisse de Prenier at 2,350m.

You now go down the south slope, first through grassland and then forest.

3:00

Pass the Cabane de Prenier on your right. After a short climb, you come onto the shoulder of land separating the Vallon de Prenier from the Ravin de la Clapière. From here, you will be able to see the path running all the way along the side of the mountain.

Warning Although the path has been restored by the ONF, it passes over steep falls and crumbling rock. For this reason, it may be necessary to take extra care, particularly in rainy weather.

Walk down from here to the Cabane du Talon.

Cabane du Talon
(See map ref 2)
1,920m
Detour *5hrs*
BAYASSE

2:00 ⌂
1,793m
The route is marked by a line of dashes on the map.

Detour see left. From the Cabane du Talon, the route follows the right bank of the Torrent de Bouchier upstream. Just as you leave the wooded area, take the footpath which goes off to the left and zig-zags up to the Col du Talon.

Col du Talon
2,414m

Now, take the path on the northern slope which passes by the Font de Baisse, a small col 15 minutes to the north east. From there, the path descends past the sheepfolds of Petit Talon towards Saint-Laurent which is on the road to the Col de la Cayolle.

3:00

From here, follow the N202 for 4 kilometres to reach Bayasse.

Warning If there is any danger of ice, the GR56 via the Petit Col de Talon (2,687m) should be avoided at the end of spring and in autumn.

BAYASSE

From the Cabane du Talon, the GR56 continues east towards the end of the Vallon de Bouchier which is blocked by a spectacular wall of rock, down which water cascades in many places. The path zig-zags up the side of this wall from the left, at one point crossing a torrent under a waterfall. The GR works its way into the cliff face and finally emerges in the hanging valley. Shortly afterwards, you come to the Cabane du Cimet, which offers a possible

2:30

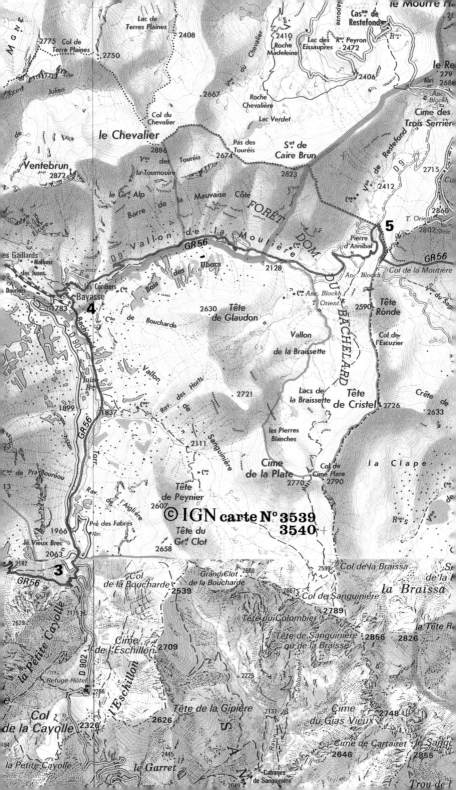

shelter. The climb continues with a further hairpin, which brings you to a path on the left coming from the Pas de l'Ane. Follow this to the right, passing a small lake, until you reach the Petit Col de Talon.

Petit Col de Talon
2,687m
Down towards the valley there are sheep pastures but the area above is very dry and stony.

1:00

Follow the path down from here, first through stony ground and then alpine meadows. Ignore the path on the left going to the Col des Esbeliouses and instead take the downhill path which passes to the left of the rock barriers which seal off the little valley. This brings you to the Cabane de la Cayolle at 2,202m. From here, the GR continues on a new dirt road. 50 metres after the first left-hand bend, take a path on the right which crosses a torrent. Continue on the left until you reach the junction with the Sentier Départemental No. 1 to the Col de la Cayolle. You now go down to the left on a path shared by the two walks until you come to the Route du Col de la Cayolle.

Route du Col de la Cayolle (ex N202)
(See map ref 3)

1:15

To reach the Refuge de Bayasse, go left down a footpath which cuts across the zig-zags of the road. This brings you to a road bridge, which you cross. Shortly afterwards, you leave the road again to your right. The GR56 crosses the road once more and now takes the old Col de la Cayolle road, which runs parallel to the new one along the Torrent du Bachelard.

BAYASSE
(See map ref 4)
1,793m

A wooden cross marks the point where the GR crosses the torrent over a temporary foot bridge. The route then continues along the right bank to Bayasse.

2:30

From the gîte, take the road which goes up the Vallon de la Moutière. 200 metres after the first left-hand hairpin, go off to your right on the old mule track which passes between low stone walls. After 10 minutes, this will bring you back to the new road at a point where it crosses a torrent. You now follow the gravelled road till you come to a right hand hairpin. Here, take the old road which continues straight ahead. As you come onto a plateau, take the tarmac road on the right to reach the Col de la Moutière.

Col de la Moutière
(See map ref 5)
2,454m

1:15

Col de Colombart
2,539m

Detour *1hr 15mins*
BOUSIÉYAS
⌂
(See map ref 7)

0:40

Col de la Blanche
2,493m

1:00

Col de la Colombière
(See map ref 6)
2,237m

1:00

20 metres before reaching the Col de la Moutière, the GR turns left off the road along a path leading to La Bonette. It veers back to the right above a rocky outcrop and virtually level going then brings you to the Col de Colombart.

Detour see left. Anyone wishing to do so can now go directly down the other slope to Bousiéyas, along a well-defined footpath with waymarkers. At the end of the track, cross over to the left bank of the torrent and follow the marked path through pasture until you come to the dirt road outside Bousiéyas.

From the Col de Colombart, the GR climbs to the top of a knoll and then follows the ridge down to the south, picking its way round boulders. You now come to the Crête de la Rougne (2,676m) and, from the summit, descend the north slope to the Col de la Blanche.

A path goes all along the sandstone ridge of the Cimes de la Blanche (2,534m). Follow the path to Pointe Giassin (2,429m). From here, there is a choice of routes down to the Col de la Colombière, one by a steep path through scree and another down the south slope across gullies.

This is a junction with the GR5, which shares the route north to Bousiéyas with the GR56. To the south, it is a walk of 1 hour and 45 minutes to Saint-Dalmas-le-Selvage where you can find hotels, restaurants and shops.

The GR5 and the GR56 follow the same route to Fouillouze.

The GR now goes north to take a path which zig-zags down, veering south west to cross the high valley of l'Issias. After crossing a flat shelf, the path descends until you cross the Torrent de Rio. Here the dirt road strikes north west and then turns right to cross the bridge over the Tinée. Join the road here and walk up to the hamlet of Bousiéyas.

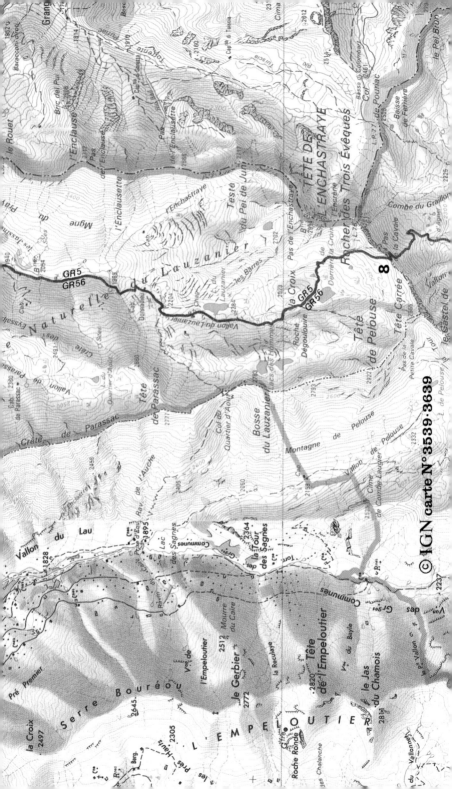

BOUSIÉYAS

(See map ref 7)

1,883m

1:15

Col des Fourches

2,261m

2:00

Pas de la Cavale

(See map ref 8)

2,711m

3:35

LARCHE

(See map ref 9)

1,675m

3:00

As you leave the gîte, immediately take the track which rises out of the village from a starting point opposite the old communal oven. After 100 metres, turn right on a footpath which climbs to the Camp des Fourches. The path passes at a tangent to two hairpins on the road and cuts across the next to bring you to the Col des Fourches.

The path descends from here in a north north-easterly direction, eventually reaching a group of barns at the end of the Vallon de Salso Moreno. Continuing in the same direction, the GR mounts the ridge which separates the Vallon de la Gypière to the west from the Val de Salso Moreno to the south east.

Upstream from the Lacs d'Agnel, the path climbs through an area of scree, ending with two hairpins in the steepest section below the Pas de la Cavale.

On the northern slope, the path turns right before passing along the right- hand shore of Lac de Derrière la Croix and then the left bank of the Vallon du Lauzanier. Going past the Lac de Lauzanier on the right, you pass the Cabane de Lauzanier and then the Cabane de Donadieu. Staying on the same bank, you come eventually to the end of the great Lauzanier plain.

The GR now follows the left bank of the Ubayette till it reaches Pont Rouge (1,907m). From the same bank, it then takes the dirt road going down to Larche.

From the gîte, cross the Torrent de Rouchouze and then, immediately after the customs post, follow the tarmac road to the right. Where the road ends, an extension track has been bulldozed through to the commune's water catchment. Slightly beyond this point, the path climbs in a series of tight hairpins on the left (west). After the hairpins, the slope becomes gradually less steep. At a wide bend where the road turns into the Vallon de Rouchouze, branch off to the left (west) on a steep path. This brings you to a large rock which you pass round on the right. (The spring here is the last water before the col.) The climb now continues across the side of the mountain until you come to open grassland with only a slight gradient. Beyond the grass, the GR zig-zags up a projecting hump to a stony slope. After going north across the side of the slope, the path again climbs in hairpins up to the Col de Mallemort.

Col de Mallemort
2,558m

The descent is by the military road which passes a derelict barracks. At a bend 1 kilometre further on, leave the road to the right and follow the arrows. You descend through pastures at a slight angle across the slope which then levels out at the crossing of the Torrent du Pinet. Now, climb across the slope to pick up the track from Fort Saint-Ours.

1:15

The GR now follows a broad ridge across grassland, passing the Lac du Vallonet on the left (west). It crosses and then recrosses the torrent. The route passes a hump-shaped projection and then carries on along the side of the slope, bringing you to the Col du Vallonnet.

Col du Vallonnet
(See map ref 10)
2,515m

Skirt round this projecting hump (2,607m) on the left (west) and then follow the path down through alpine meadows in a generally north westerly direction. The path crosses the Ravin de Fouillouze by a wooden bridge and then continues along the right bank of the Bal de Fouillouze. You arrive at the village of Fouillouze from upstream and have to cross the torrent by bridge.

1:30

FOUILLOUZE

1,900m

The GR5 and the GR56 divide at this point, the GR5 continuing towards the Col Girardin and Le Queyras. The two routes branch off from each other at the chapel in the centre of the village.

The GR56 crosses the bridge over the Torrent de Baragne and then continues along the left bank. The route follows the hillside, first on a footpath and then on a wide track with yellow and blue waymarkers as far as La Petite Serenne. After crossing a broad shelf, the GR heads north into a small depression and then turns west before dropping down to the Ubaye.

1:00

© IGN carte N° 3538·3638 3539·3639

It now follows the right bank of the river west south-west until it reaches the Pont de l'Estrech.

Pont de l'Estrech
1,453m

After crossing the bridge over the Ubaye, you have two alternatives:
1. To avoid the village of Saint-Paul-sur-Ubaye by following the cross-country ski-run along the torrent and then joining the GR6 at the footbridge over the Riou Mounal upstream from Saint-Paul.
2. To follow the main route which climbs up to the road and then follows it westwards to the village of Saint-Paul-sur-Ubaye.

0:30

SAINT-PAUL-SUR-UBAYE
⌂ ⌂ ✕ ⚓ ▬
1,470m
Meals are served all day at the cross-country ski hostel. Junction with the GR6.

The Tour de l'Ubaye ends at this point.

THE PANORAMIQUE DU MERCANTOUR

Walk 4

A way from the summer hubbub of the Mediterranean coast, the GR52A travels along the perimeter of the Parc National du Mercantour. Unlike the high mountain routes, it makes no great physical demands on walkers; rather it will introduce the walker to the warm and little known Haut-Pays, while providing views over the peaks of the Alps and revealing an architectural and historical heritage.

From the Col de Tende - with its history of wildly vacillating fortunes, and its old road with 48 hairpin bends, an actual classified historical monument - to the Col de Larche, coming out from Haute Provence to Piémont, the walker will time and again be awe-struck by the uniqueness of these surroundings and its testimonies to man's achievements.

Such achievements are not only shown by the area's remarkable historical and architectural heritage, such as Tende and La Brigue, fiefs of the turbulent Lascari family, or the monumental village of Saorge, but also by the barns of the Haute-Tinée and the 'casouns' of La Maglia, wonderful examples of how the functional can also be beautiful; or the hamlet of Tourres in the Val d'Entraunes, a perfectly preserved image of the past with its stone houses roofed with larch shingles; or again it will be the superb fortifications of Colmars-les-Alpes, in which the ingenuity of the builder involved even imitating the mountain, to obtain better protection.

And, from the Vallée de la Roya, from which you can glimpse the sea, as far as the extraordinary torrential erosion of the Tuébi; from Valdeblore, a hanging glacial plateau to the Col des Champs, the historical boundary between France and the *comté* of Nice; from the magnificence of Sospel's past to the sterling resoluteness of the villages of Roure and Roubion - one could go on and on. You have to see it all.

The Haut-Pays du Mercantour

The Mercantour (2,772m), which has given its name to the southernmost massif in the range, is not the peak of the massif - which is, in fact, the Argentera (3,297m), situated in Italian territory. This benign usurpation is due to the fact that, seen from the south and chiefly from the coast, from which virtually the whole range is visible, by a quirk of perspective, it completely obscures its rival and thus appears to be the highest peak.

The ancient rocks forming this massif (chiefly granite and gneiss) were thrust up at the end of the tertiary (Miocene) phase, during the second alpine period. Erosion of the sediment covering them, more particularly the sliding of this covering during the slow upheaval, resulted in the formation of a combination of uplands and mountains, mostly of limestone and facing the bare crystalline range, of much greater surface area and extremely contrasting relief. The glacial phases of the quaternary period refashioned all of it, chiselling the high parts and planing down the valleys, or submerging the few flat surfaces under moraines and fluvio-glacial alluvial deposits.

The mountainous mass lies approximately north north-west/south south-east. Very deep valleys bring air to the massif, and lend distinctive character to the various parts of the region from east to west. The Roya, together with the Bevera, offers the shortest route between the Po plain and the Mediterranean; then, in turn, you come upon the Vésubie and the Tinée, which, not far away from each other, pour into the Var, having forced their way through spectacular gorges and transverse escarpments, shutting off the high country to the south. The Var (in its upper reaches) and the Verdon follow the general north - south direction of the lie of the land and cut immense valleys through fragile rocks (marl and schists).

Everywhere, the erosion of torrents has left deep traces (Vallée du Tuébi in the Haut-Var, the evocatively named Vallon des Ruinas, to Saint-Sauveur-sur-Tinée) adding to the contrasting evolution of the rocky material to create blunt reliefs, and to the very marked changes of level which accentuate the variety of rock formation.

The climatic conditions are very clearly Mediterranean, but greatly tempered by the effects of the altitude and, in the south east part of the region, by the proximity of the sea (less than 15 kilometres away as the crow flies); thus, with this combination of relief and climate, you get a very noticeable stratification of the vegetation, sometimes over very short distances. In a few kilometres, you can pass from the Mediterranean belt through the hilly one to the mountain and even subalpine one: from the olive tree and the cystus to the fir and the spruce in just a few hours' walking!

To this, add, as in all mountain environments in the temperate regions, the distinct contrast between the sunny slopes (adret) and those in shadow (ubac) which are conducive either to sparse populations of bushy rather than arboreal vegetation, or to beautiful forests of fir and spruce, known today as 'black woods', because of their sombre appearance.

People had to make the best of such difficult conditions, if they were to survive through their own virtual self-sufficiency. You have to remember that if, during the bad season, the high valleys were cut off from the coast between November and April, the return of good weather was no guarantee that communications would be easy, as journeys could only be made over the ridges and transverse cols, the valley bottoms, particularly in the lower parts of water courses, being impassable even to the most minimal traffic.

Every scrap of land was consequently pressed into service, from the gardens established on the poor alluvion which had not been carried off, to the high altitude terraces, a piling up of poor 'restanques' rising to 1,600 - 1,700 metres, clinging to the immensely stiff slopes, buttressed by low stone walls, perpetually under repair (the lower part of the right bank of the Vallon de la Guerche in Isola is a quite extraordinary example of this working of the slopes). Fortunately, there were, and still are, mountain pastures, offering the only hope of survival for these agro-pastoral societies, which, formerly dependent on cattle, now rely on sheep and goats.

Above these valleys bereft of farmlands and with their 'badland' slopes fretted with ravines, there suddenly opens out, to the great surprise of the walker, wide green pasturelands, where you might easily come across several thousand sheep.
(The plateau of La Céva above La Roya near Fontan, the Vallon de Longon above the Tinée, near Roure, the Col de Champs above Var in the Val d'Entraunes all offer splendid examples of this.) Usually, the flocks are let out to pasture in summer, as nowadays, except in exceptional conditions, mountain farming is an activity that is rapidly disappearing, and this is evident throughout the countryside: abandoned irrigation canals, crumbling or vanished terrace retaining walls, chalets and barns abandoned or in ruins; and the cleared slopes are overrun once more by trees and shrubs (durmast oaks and broom, for example).

It is in this region, with its abundance and variety of environments, where considerable differences in level between the summits and the gouged out valleys create suitable walking conditions a few kilometres from the overcrowded coastline, that the Sentier Panoramique de Mercantour, far and wide, draws its winding course, over almost 200 kilometres.

Between the Cols de Tende (1,871m) and Larche (1,991m), only some sixty kilometres from each other as the crow flies, and which are, remember, the only alpine passes (along with the Montgenèvre in the Hautes-Alpes) open to traffic to Italy all the year round, the Sentier Panoramique du Mercantour represents a new approach to tourism in the Alpes-Maritimes and the Alpes de Haut-Provence.

In fact, if the high mountain area, corresponding roughly to the Parc National du Mercantour which is crossed by the GR5 and GR52 joining Lake Geneva to the Mediterranean, enjoys ever-increasing publicity, the rest of the Haute-Pays, still only known to a few, also deserves to be discovered. Situated in the peripheral area of the national park, the Sentier Panoramique du Mercantour will be able to make a considerable contribution to the economic life of the communes of which it is constituted, since all the stops are centred on the villages and hamlets providing lodging and essential shops.

WALK 4

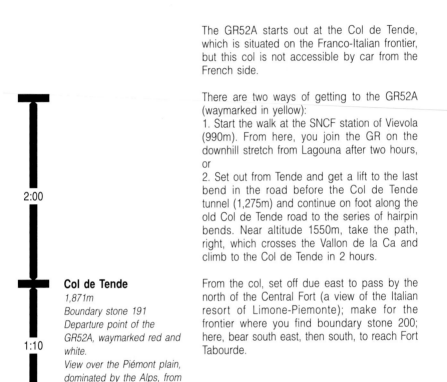

The GR52A starts out at the Col de Tende, which is situated on the Franco-Italian frontier, but this col is not accessible by car from the French side.

There are two ways of getting to the GR52A (waymarked in yellow):
1. Start the walk at the SNCF station of Vievola (990m). From here, you join the GR on the downhill stretch from Lagouna after two hours, or
2. Set out from Tende and get a lift to the last bend in the road before the Col de Tende tunnel (1,275m) and continue on foot along the old Col de Tende road to the series of hairpin bends. Near altitude 1550m, take the path, right, which crosses the Vallon de la Ca and climb to the Col de Tende in 2 hours.

2:00

Col de Tende
1,871m
Boundary stone 191
Departure point of the GR52A, waymarked red and white.
View over the Piémont plain, dominated by the Alps, from Mont Viso to Mont Rose.

1:10

From the col, set off due east to pass by the north of the Central Fort (a view of the Italian resort of Limone-Piemonte); make for the frontier where you find boundary stone 200; here, bear south east, then south, to reach Fort Tabourde.

The Col de Tende
A favoured frontier between the Po Plain and the southern face of the southern Alps, the Col de Tende is a place steeped in history. The easiest crossing between the Piémont and the gateways to the Mediterranean, the Col de Tende was an object of envy from all sides. The local nobility, the Lascari (well established in Tende) subjected its trading to their whims, and it was also important to the Dukes of Savoy who, from 1575, controlled the Comté de Tende. The pass was of vital importance for the very lucrative transport of salt and all manner of goods, and was improved by the Dukes of Savoy. In 1616, the first track suitable for vehicles between the sea and Piémont was finished. It gradually became a road, the process being completed with the drilling of a tunnel in 1883 (after 9 years' toil) to facilitate winter crossings.

The forts which mark the start of this route are a reminder of the turbulent and chequered history of this perpetually coveted region.

Fort Tabourde
1,982

0:45

Baisse de Lagouna
1,677m

1:45

TENDE
🏠 ⌂ 🚉 ⛺ 📶
816m
The feast of Saint-Éloi, patron of shepherds, gives rise on the 2nd Sunday of July to a picturesque cavalcade of mules in dress harness.

1:00

Col de Loubayre
997m

0:30

LA BRIGUE
🏠 ⌂ 🍴 🚉 📶
765m
A Romanesque church with Lombard belfry; in the town many 13th and 16th century door lintels embellished with the green slate of the Roya.

1:30

Baisse de Peloune
1,279m

0:30

Col de Géréon
1,254m
Marked by a cross which may have disappeared.

1:30

Still walking due south and following the ridge, you reach the Cime du Tavan, then descend to Baisse de Lagouna.

From Vievola station (990m), join the N204, pass beneath the railway and take the 'Valléen de Tende' path. At waymark 331, leave it to climb (north east) past the Barre du Caïron to the Lagouna descent.

The GR takes the path left, skirts Mont Court on its east flank, then descends (south east) to the remains of the Tailladan barns (1,250m); goes over a small crest (height reference 1,115) and still descending south, reaches the town of Tende, near the station.

The GR leaves the town going south, following the right bank of the Roya; a little further on, you cross the river over a small bridge, then cross the N204 to the right of a sawmill (782m). Then take the forest road rising in hairpin bends to the Col de Loubayre.

From the col, descend south, then east down a rocky path to the D43, which you take east, to enter the town of La Brigue.

Leave the village heading west, then turn south to climb through the Riodore locality on the Baisse d'Arpèse (1,288m). Still heading south, you join the Baisse de Peloune.

Cross onto the east face of the Cime de Durasca, to reach Col de Géréon

The GR crosses the barely marked col and takes the forest road due south; it crosses the top of the Vallon de Groa and further on arrives at the often dry Fontaine de Vastète (1492), where it turns west to reach the Baisse de Lugo.

111

History of Tende and La Brigue

Tende and La Brigue have always been a part of the *Comté* of Nice. At the time of the plebiscite of 15 April 1861, which gave its blessing to the return of the latter to France by virtue of the Franco-Sardinian treaty of 25 March 1860, the two communes had unanimously voted in France's favour. However, Napoléon III, out of courtesy, allowed King Victor-Emmanuel II to hunt in the Mercantour massif, and that is how the upper valleys of La Roya, La Vésubie and La Tinée remained under Italian rule for 87 years. Thanks both to the tenacity of its people and the strong backing of the French Foreign Minister, Georges Bidault, this region was once more joined to France by the Peace Treaty of 10 February. Nevertheless, of their own free will, in the plebiscite of October 1947, the people of Tende and La Brigue offered themselves to France by a vote of 2,603 to 218.

It was no more than the righting of an anomaly in the line of the frontier of 1860, which descended over the French side of the Alps. The new frontier normally follows the skyline formed by the natural boundary marking between the two countries, passing through Mont Rognosa, Mont Clapier, the Col de Tende, the Monts Marguareis, Saccarel and Pitravecchia.

On the way down to La Brigue from the Col du Loubayre, the walker will come across a valley of fruit trees: sturdy little trees, neat rows of peach, pear, apple and plum on sunny terraces, warmed also by the dry-stone walls supporting the successive levels. Rounding a bend in the path, the traveller is struck by the beauty of some of these walls, and the meticulous arrangement of the small stones, where necessary supported by a long stone or large round pebble from the river. These orchards, wrested from the mountain, are master-pieces born of patience and character, and bear testimony to the desperate struggle of past generations to earn a living from this countryside.

Opposite the southern slope of the valley, which is given over to orchards and apiaries (honey is one of La Brigue's riches), the north slope spreads out its dark forests of pine, fir and larch to the bottom of the valleys, and marches on the mountains, invading them with their dark forest names: Black Valley, Milky Agaric Wood. Discover the village of La Brigue on the even terrain, with its paved streets, its arcades along the Rio Secco, its antique doorways topped by lintels, its crooked belfry, its coloured tower and its church, famous for its sixteenth century altar-pieces. On the banks of the Levensa, cross the peculiar right-angled bridge, the Pont de Coq, to join the road from which, beyond La Brigue, you can gaze at Mont Bego, the peak of Les Merveilles.

Baisse de Lugo
1,475m

Over ground which is now level, continue heading south; 400 metres further on, you meet the Fontaine aux Chiens.

Fontaine aux Chiens
(frequently dry).
Detour *2hrs 30mins*
FONTAN
🏠 ✕ ⚖ Å
425m

0:20

From the Fontaine aux Chiens, the GR climbs (south) as far as Baisse d'Anan.

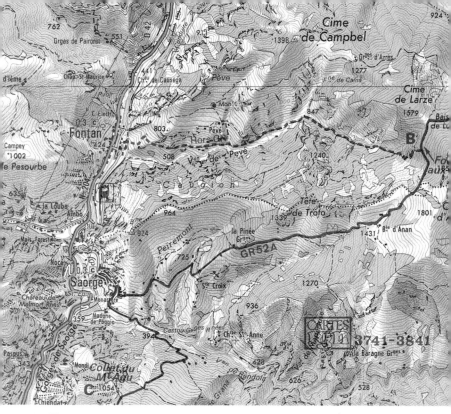

Situated on the N204 in the
Vallée de la Roya.
Take the footpath waymarked
yellow in the Vallon de l'Eau
Froide.

Baisse d'Anan
1,555m

2:20

Go south west, down a poorly marked out path
(a lot of sheep tracks) as far as a shoulder,
where the Anan barns stand: the GR then finds
a better marked path which it takes westward.
You pass the Pinée barns, walk through the

Baisse de Lugo

Here, you are met by a view over the Massif de l'Argentera and, due west, over
the most famous heights of the region (Bégo, Abysse, La Cime du Diable). The
large valleys glimpsed to the west (Merveilles, Caramagne) are of glacial origin
and certain of them, like the Vallée de Fontanalbe, are very characteristic of this
type of valley. The profusion of lakes is the result of the passage of glaciers,
leaving in their wake many glacial thresholds, depressions in which the water
remained trapped. The range terminates in the south with the most recently
formed massif, the Authion, an area of grass and forest that is one of the
richest pasturelands in the area.

mountain meadows of Peyremont (700m) to
descend (south, then west). You go past a
monastery and enter the village of Saorge.

SAORGE

🏠 ⌂ ✕ ⚖ ⚏

520m

*An extraordinary-looking
village with houses facing
south and rising in steps.
Below, lies the spectacle of
the Gorges du Roya. Outside
the village is the
Romanesque church of the
Madone del Poggio, with its
Romanesque belfry in the
Lombard style.*

2:00

The GR leaves Saorge along the road passing
the Madone del Poggio. Continue as far as the
hairpin bend in this road (waymark 161). Go
down to the Bendola bridge, cross it and climb
a good path up to Baoussoun. Still climbing,
and after walking through a forest, you arrive at
the small Mont Agu col.

Saorge

Past La Brigue, there is a gentle climb up to the Baisse d'Anan, from where the
path descends to Saorge. Here there are mountain torrents, valleys, plateaux,
and distinctive alpine scenery on all sides. Beyond La Roya and its cliffs,
perches the village of Saorge. Facing it is a valley where the people of Saorge
have their gardens, stables, barns, mountain pastures and forest - the Cayros
valley. Similarly, Fontan and Bergue Inférieure and Supérieure draw a large part
of their livelihood from their terraced plots, the vines and mountain pastures of
La Ceva. That is the broad canvas, but let us take a look at the day-to-day life
of the place. Saorge is a town built around its olive press. Here, we find the
purple 'chiappes', the steep, venetian-coloured façades, the clock-towers of
multi-coloured mosaic, the distant silhouette of the pearl grey clock-tower of the
Madone del Poggio. The alleys of the upper and lower parts of the town (two
different worlds) are paved and cool, even in summer. The monastery is richly
decorated with frescoes which are currently being restored by the Franciscan
monks, masons and painters. Here, we have the small flagged squares, houses
with the wooden balconies on which garlic, figs, thyme and maize are set out
to dry. Culinary tradition is still very much alive in Saorge: try the 'picore'
(brioche with raisins and orange water), the small soused, black olives, the
'tourtons' (tomato fritters), the 'quiques' (green pasta with wild spinach).

From Saorge, you are entering olive country. The grey colouring of the olive
trees characterizes the Mediterranean countryside, and covers whole swathes of
mountain.

The olive tree has long played a major rôle in the local economy: the
production of olives, the local oil presses and the carving of the wood. After a
period of recession, due to poor overall economic conditions and a blight that
has ravaged the olive groves, its cultivation is now picking up again.

In this very rugged countryside, the olive trees are grown on terraces,
witnesses to the back-breaking toil of generations of forbears.

Collet du Mont Agu
1,065m
View-point at the wayside cross, near by.

3:00

BREIL-SUR-ROYA
ⓗ ✕ ⚒ ⚠ 🚂
290m

2:00

COL DE BROUIS
ⓗ
879m
Intersected by the D2204.

1:20

Col de Pérus
659m

2:00

SOSPEL
350m
ⓗ ⌂ ✕ ⚒ ⚠ 🚂
🚇
The GR52, the alternative route to the GR5, passes through here on its way from Saint-Dalmas-Valdeblore and heading for Menton. See Walk 2.
The GR de Pays de Huit

Cross onto the west flank of Mont Agu. After quite a long descent, you join the Sentier Valléen de la Roya at a wayside cross (505m - waymark 154).

The route of the GR is shared southward by the Sentier Valléen, as far as waymark 153.

In the Ornéglia locality, continue south up an easy climb.Cross the Vallon de Zouayné. Turn right (west, then south) to arrive in the middle of Breil-sur-Roya.

To leave Breil-sur-Roya, return to the tunnel under the railway line: then, as you leave it, take the road left (south) leading to the Chapelle Madone des Grâces. The road gives way to a track which turns south west and climbs into a forest until it reaches Col de Brouis.

At the Col de Brouis (war memorial), take the Piène-Haute track (east, then south) as far as the Col de Paula (739m, stones marking the old frontier with Italy). Turn east and skirt the Tête de Bassera south, then west, and descend into the Vallée de la Bassera. Follow the left edge down, then cross over and climb to Col de Pérus.

Cross the D2204, skirt the top of the Vallon de Mergil or Pérus, and you meet the Vallon de Callecastagna or Figuetta. Cross it and, 800 metres further up, leave it to climb to the Baisse du Mont Agaisen (666m). Continue along the south slope, first following the zig-zagging road, then along a path which descends to Sospel.

The GR52A leaves Sospel along the small Bérouf road, following the left bank of the Bévéra until it ends. From here (road sign), descend along a valley, cross the Bévéra and the D2566. The GR follows a track climbing to the hamlet of Saint Vincent.

*Vallées also passes through
Sospel on its way from Breil
(Roya) to Saint-Cézaire
(Siagne).*
*Sospel lies at the confluence
of the Bévéra and Merlanson
torrents. A summer holiday
town situated in a
depression, cultivated in
terraces and surrounded by
stark looking mountains. The
Bévéra divides the town in
two; the medieval bridge with
its two arches and its central
tower, damaged in 1944, has
been rebuilt.*

3:30

The GR winds through a few hairpin bends
and reaches the wooded plateau of Piastra,
where it arrives at the foot of the Cime de
Pénas. Here, there are two possible routes:
1. You can follow the GR flanking the Cime de
Pénas, west, and after a stiff climb, reach the
'Pas de la Capelette' footpath;
2. You can follow the path waymarked yellow
(route offering spectacular views, but not
advisable in bad weather) which climbs to the
Cime de Pénas (1,018m). Here, you look down
over the Pion Gorges.

The marly limestone, dating from the end of the
first secondary, has been hewn by the water to
create this landscape, so fretted with
spectacular folds.

On the left edge of these gorges, you see a
forest of Ostrya (also known as 'hop
hornbeam') which covers the valley to its
utmost tip. It is a typical tree of the mountains
of the eastern Mediterranean.

The whole of this region, difficult for access
and possessing few roads, is particularly rich
in all manner of wildlife (birds, small mammals,
reptiles and rodents).

Continue bearing north over the wooded and
rocky crest (no footpath) to rejoin the GR at
Pas de la Capelette.

Pas de la Capelette
962m

2:30

The GR follows the ridge (north), to an altitude
of 1050m. Here, take the track on the east
flank of the Tête de Barlou east, to join the
forest track leading to the Chapelle Saint-
Michel (932m). Continue north east, leave the
winding track and descend to the village of
Moulinet.

MOULINET
⌂ ✗ ☖ ▭
801m

2:45

Leave Moulinet heading north to climb along a
gravel track to Castellet; the GR winds west
north-west, passes the Sueil houses on the left
and takes the crest path climbing to Baisse de
Patronel.

Baisse de Patronel
1,607m

Continue climbing north. The path runs parallel
to the D2566 road (Peïra-Cava-Turini).

If the high temperature indicates the proximity of the Côte d'Azur, the typical, predominantly shrubby vegetation in its turn, shows the influence of the Mediterranean climate. You will recognize species such as cystus, broom, juniper and a variety of aromatic plants; the fir and olive provide a little shade. The observant walker will glimpse the fleeting form of a frightened rabbit, innumerable in these parts. Finally, on the slopes of Mont Gros, you can see the southernmost fir forest in France.

0:45

You are now coming to the part of the route closest to the coastline. The altitude drops; in fine weather the sea is clearly visible and it is often possible to glimpse Corsica.

You skirt the Cime de la Calmette, west, pass beneath the cables of a ski-tow, to arrive at a forest house and descend to the Col de Turini.

COL DE TURINI
⌂ ✗

1,607m
Crossroads

2:45

At the Col de Turini on the GR52A, waymarked red and white, takes the forest track (west) situated below the Peïra-Cava. Follow it for about 7 kilometres up to the Cime de l'Escaletta, and on the crest, you come across a track descending in a series of hairpin bends to the Sainte-Élizabeth torrent (520m). Climb back onto the right bank of the torrent to reach the village of La Bollène-Vésubie.

LA BOLLÈNE-VÉSUBIE
Ⓗ ⌂ 🚋 🚌

690m

2:20

Leave La Bollène along the Flaut road, but after a wayside cross quite close by, turn left onto a descending path to cross the Vallon de la Planchette. Climb once again, cutting across the road several times to reach the Fort de Flaut (866m).

Bearing north, take the path descending and crossing the Gordolasque. Climb the opposite slope and, after crossing two roads, you arrive at Belvédère.

BELVÉDÈRE
Ⓗ ✗ 🚋

830m

Alternative route via the crests. At the place, called 'La Colla', there is an alternative unwaymarked route which goes to Saint-Martin-Vésubie by the crests. In spite of the quite high altitude (highest point 2,300m), this alternative route presents no problems - but beware of storms on the crests.

The Forêt de Turini

The Forêt de Turini is one of the most beautiful in the region. Composed chiefly of firs and locally of beeches, it conveys the atmosphere of the great forests of the north. The forest plays a major rôle in the balance of nature, consolidating the land, protecting against erosion, and preventing avalanches by retaining the snow. It provides plentiful food supplies and a safe haven for countless animals.

In these mountain regions, the forest often also constitutes a major source of income for communes. Regular felling, scheduled long in advance, enables communes, otherwise poor, to survive. The forest is therefore a vital element in mountain life and deserves our respect and care.

From the Col de Turini, the route crosses a very steep north-facing slope, covered by a rich forest of spruce and fir, reminding us that the mountain climate of the Alpes-Maritimes is very humid, at least in the eastern part of the department.

The atmosphere changes abruptly at the level of the Cime de l'Escaletta. Here, the path crosses a forest environment which is completely artificial. The whole of this route runs through often dense forest, and landscaped clearings are few. Nevertheless, it is often possible to catch an occasional glimpse of the middle region of the Vésubie Valley.

Allow eight and a half hours to get to Saint-Martin-Vésubie, with no stopping or resting. It is possible to go down from La Baisse de Férisson to the Madone de Fenestre CAF refuge (1,900).

3:40

The unwaymarked alternative route takes the small road leading to the Blancon barns; a footpath cuts across the first few of its hairpin bend en route to the Croix de Serre; you regain the road, which you follow to the next hairpin bend, and here take a path which avoids the road. At an altitude of about 1,500 metres, cut across the road to take an unmade-up track climbing, parallel with this road, up to the cowshed at Férisson.

Vacherie de Férisson
1,910m

1:10

Continue bearing north, then west on a very good track climbing to Baisse de Férisson.

Baisse de Férisson
2,254m
A large wooden cross, view over the Cirque de Fenestre.
Detour *1hr 30mins*

3:45
REFUGE DE LA MADONE DE FENESTRE
1,900m

The alternative route follows a path on the south slope of the Férisson/La Palu crest, bearing west. You cross the crest south of the Cime de la Palu and the path descends south, then west as far as the Saint-Antoine bridge, where you rejoin the GR52A and follow it until you reach the town of Saint-Martin-Vésubie.

CAF refuge located at the end of the D94 road climbing from St-Martin-Vésubie; a warden in summer.
The GR52 St-Martin-Valdeblore/Menton passes through here;

Saint-Martin-Vésubie
964m

BELVÉDÈRE
⌂ ✕ ⚓
830m

2:30

The GR passes close to a cemetery at the Chapelle du Planet and, a little further on, arrives at the fork with the road leading to the Blancon barns.

In the locality of 'La Colla', the GR52A does not take the small road leading to the Blancon barns, but takes a path below the road climbing up to a column (1128m). From here it descends to a bridge which you cross to climb to Berthemont-les-Bains.

BERTHEMONT-LES-BAINS
⌂
936m

The GR52A crosses the D72, then takes a path which crosses the Vallon de Vernet and climbs upward in very tight hairpin bends to reach a shoulder at 1296m. You then descend due south.

The view
On the Biolet plateau, at the foot of a gnarled oak tree, stop and take in the surrounding view. To the south, below you, Berthemont; further off, the village of Belvédère glints in the sunlight; finally, at the bottom of the valley, is La Bollène-Vésubie. To the west, the forest of Molune stretches its black mantle of fir and spruce as far as the foot of Caïre Gros, while, perched on a rocky spur, the small village of Venanson looks out over the valley.

To the north west, the horizon is obscured by the limestone summits of the Balme de la Fréma and the Pépoiri, the last bastions of sedimentary rock in the valley.

On the crest of La Pénète, a conduit, drilled through 1,800 metres to a drop in height of 710 metres, carries water harnessed from the torrents of Boréon, La Madone and Gordolasque to the hydro-electric station.

To the north, facing us, stretch the Plague Fields. Here, in 1528, during the terrible plague epidemic, the sick were placed in quarantine. The route continues through the undergrowth of a chestnut grove which today, sadly, is no longer tended.

At the ridge named Serre de Bous (beef backbone), a small wooden bench invites you to rest a while; down in the valley, you can see the best arable land, glacial deposits covered in Saint-Martin-Vésubie alluvial soil.

In the middle of a hay field, stands a mass of rock left by the ice. A Saint-Martin legend has it that it was witches who must have rolled it there, while playing pelota on the slopes of Mont Archas, under the light of a full moon.

A thermal spa on a small plateau, where some ten sulphur and soda springs gush, at an approximate temperature of 30°C.

2:30

Known from antiquity on account of a visit by the Empress Salomine, who came to the baths to take the cure in the year 261, this thermal spa is still in use today.

SAINT-MARTIN-VÉSUBIE
🏠 ⌂ ✕ ⚏ ▬ ⋏

964m

A health and summer resort, Saint-Martin is built at the confluence of the Boréon and the Madone de Fenestre; it was a large town in the 16th century, due to its position on the 'salt route'. The brick-lined canal which crosses the town was built in 1420, and used to serve as the town's main drainage system.

1:45

COL SAINT-MARTIN-LA-COLMIANE
🏠 ✕

1,500m

A forest track, under construction, will enable you to avoid the route by the shoulder: pay close attention to the waymarking.

The GR takes the farm track flanking the mountainside amid oaks and white heather.

Taking the farm track, now a road, you arrive at the bridge of Saint-Antoine, which you cross to enter Saint-Martin-Vésubie.

Leave the town, heading north along the right bank of the Boréon; in the Saint-Nicholas quarter, you find a footpath. You follow it west and, 100 metres further on, it turns south west to cross the Vallon du Vernet: this is an old Roman road which, via the col, linked the Emilia Way, rising along the northern face of the Alps, with the Aurelia Julia Way from Pisa to Fréjus.

The track climbs up in the shade of nut-trees. After gaining a little height, the high range of the Alpes-Maritimes obscures the horizon. This is the watershed and has been the frontier between France and Italy since 1945. It is also the private hunting ground of past kings of Italy. This hub of the national hunting reserve established in 1948 (and since 1979 included in the central area of the Parc National du Mercantour) is the favoured sanctuary of chamois, ibex and wild sheep. It is a crystalline massif composed of gneiss and granite. In the valley, the dwellings, clustered together on the poor soil and the terraced plots, testify to a tough agricultural heritage. Today, the forest and coppices have taken over this once cultivated land.

You thus arrive at the D2565, which you follow to reach the nearby resort of Col Saint-Martin-la-Colmiane.

The GR52A takes a path west, below the road, from which you can see, looking northward, the imposing Baous de la Fréma ('Baou' meaning 'large rock', an enormous, Triassic, magnesian limestone block, and 'Fréma', meaning

'woman'. This name emanates from a legend associated with the grotto which opens out of the side of the mountain. An inhabitant of Valdeblore, having been tricked by the local squire, tried to tie up his wife in this grotto.

At the first fork in the road, take the path left to reach the village of Saint-Dalmas-Valdeblore.

0:30

SAINT-DALMAS-VALDEBLORE

🏠 ⌂ ⚓ ✕ 🍷 ⚰

🚌

1,290m
Alpine village taking in 3 hamlets (La Bolline, La Roche, St-Dalmas) on a glacial terrace with rich, well displayed lands, opposite the beautiful Bois Noir forest. Visit the 11th century Église de la Sainte Croix with its 9th century underground crypt. A famous historic monument: ask in the village when the key can be obtained for visiting it. Junction of the GR5 to Nice and the GR52 to Menton.

The GR5 and GR52A take the D2565 west; just after the bridge, leave the GR5, which continues along the road, and turn left onto a path descending into the Vallon de Bramafan. Follow the left edge then the Goune road as far as the small col (1,123m). Bear north east and descend, then cross the Vallon de Bramafan and rejoin the D2565 at the bend near the Église Saint-Jacques, which is one of the churches in La Bolline.

1:10

LA BOLLINE

🏠 ✕ 🍷

995m

1:10

From this bend, the GR5 and GR52A run along the Bramafan valley, then cross what formerly was the tongue of the glacier, now covered with meadow grass, and descend to cross the Gros valley (bridge at 800m). Over level ground, you reach the D2565 to Planet. Climb up the road again as far as the next bend, take the road going to the small Col de Raglas and you arrive at Rimplas.

Rimplas

1,016m
Built on a shoulder surmounted by a large fort and with the Chapelle de la Madeleine perched on a rocky needle.

1:15

The GR will take the ancient road linking the high villages of Valdeblore to Saint-Sauveur-sur-Tinée.

At the foot of the village of Rimplas, the GR continues over level terrain (north west) on the road (cut out and recently widened) through steep 'roubines'. Losing altitude, cross the Éclos and Romannier valleys.

Pass below the Chapelle St-Roche, leave the small road and take the path left, winding downhill. You regain the road, a little above the first bend; follow it to Saint-Sauveur-sur-Tinée.

SAINT-SAUVEUR-SUR-TINÉE

🏠 ⌂ ⚠ ⚓ ▭

496m

Principal town of the mid-Tinée valley. Visit the church of St-Sauveur and its clocktower dating from 1133. After the church, the GR descends to cross the Tinée and pass below the cemetery.

2:00

At the foot of the cemetery, the GR take the right-hand path which climbs through innumerable bends and intersects the road in several places. It is a steep climb to the village of Roure.

ROURE

🏠 ✗ ⚓ ▭

1,096m

A quaint village perched above the confluence of the Vionène and Tinée. The community has, in the past 120 years, lost more than half its population (currently 112 inhabitants). In the church, see the altar-piece of François Bréa (1560) depicting the Assumption of the Virgin and above the high altar, the altar-piece of Saint-Laurent and Saint-Grat of the same period. Climb to the remains of the château for the view.

3:00

The GR climbs to the Saint-Sébastien chapel, then bears north. Shortly afterwards, leave the GR5 and continue in the direction of Rougios and the north; the GR52A bears west, continues as far as the Cerise barns, crosses the Cerise ravine and continues practically as far, on the same level, and arrives at the ruins of the Basset and Pont barns.

Level with the road bridge over the Vionène, leave the path and meander downhill to meet the covered canal. Following the canal, cross the valley and climb up to return to the path following the right edge of this valley. Continue bearing north west as far as the subway, climb the easy slope and walk to the alluvial cone. Cross the Vionène. Climb up a path which you can barely make out, onto the other edge, bearing south, and follow the Vignols track as far as Roubion.

ROUBION

⚓

1,314m

1:30

Near the church, the GR52A bears west, reaches the hamlet of Vallons and climbs to Col de la Couillole.

COL DE LA COUILLOLE

🏠 ✗

1,678m

1:00

Go down into the Vallon de la Couillole following the left edge. Lower down (1,386m), return to the right edge and climb up to the Chapelle Saint-Ginie. Take the tarmac road (north), cross the Cians and, along the old road, climb up to Beuil.

BEUIL

1,450m
Downhill and cross-country ski resort.

Peaceful-looking village, once the fief of the Comtes de Beuil, bold and powerful enough to dispute hegemony with Nice over a long period. On this section, the route is dominated to the north by the stark limestone bulk of Mont Mounier, rising to 2,817m.

0:30

Cross the village from end to end, pass below the barracks and continue bearing west to reach the Col Sainte-Anne chapel.

Col Sainte-Anne

1,551m
Situated near the hamlet of Launes. Centre for cross-country skiing.

1:15

Head south of the chapel, then bear west and take the road serving the houses in Sagne. Go past an oratory (1,517m), cross the Chalandre valley (often dry) and climb the shady side up to Col des Atres (1,684m) along a good path.

Continue north west to join the road, where you see a swimming pool, then follow this road to reach the resort of Valberg.

VALBERG

1,669m
Visit the modern church with frescoes by Casarini.

1:15

Pass the Valbergame house. Shortly before an intersection, leave the road along a footpath. Bear north down an easy slope, then follow a crest bearing west.

The path then cuts across the hairpin bends of the D29 several times; at the oratory of Saint-Jacques, take this road as far as Péone.

PÉONE

1,172m
Magnesian limestone needles to the north of the village.

2:00

The GR leaves the village heading west. Shortly after the bridge over the Tuebi (right edge), the path climbs to cross the small Chardonnier road, passes below an oratory and joins the Plan track. It intersects its hairpin bends, passes in front of a drinking trough and comes out onto the Haut-Villard shoulder (1,431m). Continue bearing west, cross the ridge south of the Collet d'Aulivet (1,571m); turn due north, then west to cross the Vallon des Abbéourouns (tricky crossing, badlands). Afterwards, you reach the hamlet of Geyne without difficulty, then the hamlet of Bouchanières.

BOUCHANIÈRES
✕
1,416m

1:40

From the inn, take the road (west) climbing to the church. Leave this, and further on turn onto the path passing below the road. Cross the hamlet of Hivernasses and you end up at an intersection with the Barels track, then:

● either, at waymarking 150, descend and cross the Vallon des Roubines to meet the oratory at the small col (1,363m.)

● or follow the Barels track as far as the second ridge and descend to meet the oratory mentioned above. The path turns north and reaches the ruins of the Ginieys barns; go down and cross the Barlatte, then climb to the Richard farm and further on, you arrive at the Chapelle Saint-Antoine at the foot of Châteauneuf d'Entraunes.

CHATEAUNEUF D'ENTRAUNES
⌂
1,293m

2:00

From the Chapelle Saint-Antoine, the GR takes the path overlooking the Tourres track, to find it once again a little further on, before the hamlet of Tourres.

Tourres
1,680m
Typical mountain homes, well preserved, with shingle roofs and stone floors.

1:20

The GR continues on its route (north west) to arrive at Col des Trente Souches.

Col des Trente Souches.
2,017m
The GR skirts to the north of a depression, an old peat bog. This is a paradise for botanists, but also a museum, since it preserves plant pollens from long ago.

2:30

You cross a stream and enter a forest. The path makes a detour north, losing altitude, but remaining on the left bank of the Bourdous. You pass a rocky threshold (path cut in the wall), then at the foot of the Ravine du Brec waterfall (1,666m) there is a very tricky path. The path gives way to a forest track which you follow as far as height reference 1540, indicated by a sign of the Parc du Mercantour (drinking trough below); here, leave the track for a path, right, which descends and cuts across the winding bends in the forest track. Cross the torrent over a wooden bridge and go into the village.

ENTRAUNES
⌂ ✕ ⚓ ▭
1,251m

2:30

The GR crosses the Var and takes a path (Parc sign) climbing to Col de la Porte (passing over the rocky ridge) at 1525m. Follow the boundary of the Parc National du Mercantour, waymarked with green hexagons, climbing to Col des Champs.

Col des Champs

2,045m

Old frontier between France (Verdon side) and the Duchy of Savoy (Var side). It also

2:30

marks the boundary between the departments of the Alpes des Haute-Provence and the Alpes-Maritimes.

COLMARS

1,269m

The gîte d'étape is situated in the ramparts; enjoy wandering through the maze of streets to find it.

The red and white waymarking continues as far as Colmars; see broken line on map.

Past Colmars, the GR52A will continue into the Alpes-de-Haute-Provence, to join the GR5 at the Col de Larche.

The countryside around Colmars

The descent to Colmars passes through a succession of clearly differentiated types of countryside. There are few of the larger animals to be seen, but you do come across a large number of bird species, the direct beneficiaries of the diversity of climates, food and habitats.

From the Col des Champs, in the treeless, alpine belt, you encounter beautiful close-cropped grassland, where marmots do battle, and rough scree intersected by stark ravines; while further up, rocky ridges glower down. Each of these environments has developed its own flowers, which have managed to adapt to the conditions, each combination different, of the respective terrains.

Next, you enter a larch forest in the subalpine belt, where arolla pine and rowan grow above the undergrowth; in the clearings around the Ratery well (drinking water), you can see parallel lines, the remains of the terraces of an old nursery, and evidence of the massive reafforestation which took place at the beginning of the century. You can see that the larches are almost all of the same age and that the more arid, opposite side of the mountain, has been replanted with pitch pine.

Gradually, as you descend, you come into the highlands. The alpine meadow landscapes, carpeted with flowers and bordered with wild hedgerows - a source of food and shelter for the animals - are born of man's arduous and patient toil. Today, nature is reasserting its rights; the durmast oak is taking over the abandoned meadows, while the Norwegian pine is re-establishing itself on the poor and arid slopes.

You arrive at Colmars by way of the Fort de Savoie, from which you look out over the ramparts of the town, and further in the distance, the Fort de France. Altered by Vauban, these fortifications are a reminder that this site, now protected by a conservation order, was at one time the frontier between the Houses of Savoy and Provence.

ACCOMMODATION GUIDE

The many different kinds of accommodation in France are explained in the introduction. Here we include a selection of hotels and other addresses, which is by no means exhaustive – the hotels listed are usually in the one-star or two-star categories. We have given full postal addresses where available so bookings can be made.

There has been an explosive growth in bed and breakfast facilities (chambres d'hôte) in the past few years, and staying in these private homes can be especially interesting and rewarding. Local shops and the town hall (mairie) can usually direct you to one.

Allos (Col d')
04440 Uvernet Fours
⌂
Mr Léautaud
☎ *92.83.81.68*
☎ *92.81.12.24*

Aspremont
06790 Aspremont
⌂ *Hostellerie d'Aspremont*
Mr Camous
☎ *93.08.00.05*
⌂ *Le Saint Jean*
Mr Rubert
☎ *93.08.00.66*

Auron
06660 Saint Etienne de Tinée
⌂ *Las Donnas*
Mr Roques
☎ *93.23.00.03*

Barcelonette
04400 Barcelonette
⌂
J Chaix
☎ *92.81.01.26*

Bayasse
04440 Uvernet Fours
⌂
Mr Guinde
☎ *92.81.07.31*

Berthemont les Bains
06450 Roquebilliere
⌂ *Chalet des Alpes*
Mr Monni-Peda
☎ *93.03.51.65*

Beuil
06470 Guillaumes
⌂ *l'Escapade*
Mr Mary
☎ *93.02.31.27*

Beuil les Launes
06470 Guillaumes
⌂ *Beuil les Launes*
☎ *93.02.31.93*

Bousiéyas
06660 Saint-Dalmas-le-Selvage
⌂ *De Bousiéyas*
Mr Baboin
☎ *92.02.42.20*
☎ *90.98.36.09*

Breil sur Roya
06540 Breil sur Roya
⌂ *Castel du Roy*
Mr Huyghe
☎ *93.04.43.66*

La Brigue
06430 Tende
⌂ *Mirval*
Mr and Mme Dellepiane
☎ *93.04.63.71*

Châteauneuf d'Entraunes
06470 Guillaumes
⌂ *La Ferme du Pouss*
☎ *93.05.54.42*

Entraunes
06470 Guillaumes
⌂ *Auberge Roche Grande*
☎ *93.05.51.83*

Fontan
06540 Breuil sur Roya
⌂ *Auberge de la Roya*
Mme Tourais

☎ *93.04.50.19*

Fouillouze
04520 Saint-Paul-sur-Ubaye
⌂ *Fouillouze*
Mr Bourillon
☎ *92.84.31.16*

Jausiers
04850 Jausiers
⌂
Mr Nerenhaussen
☎ *92.84.61.34*

Larche
04540 Larche
⌂ *Au Relais d'Italie*
Mme Palluel
☎ *92.84.31.32*
⌂
Mr Pierre Lombard
☎ *92.84.30.80*

Lavercq
04340 Le Lauzet Ubaye
⌂
Mr Silve
☎ *92.85.53.09*
☎ *92.35.00.75*
☎ *94.29.57.73*

Levens
06670 Saint-Martin-du-Var
⌂ *Des Grandes Pres*
Mr Romulus
☎ *93.79.70.35*
⌂ *Malausenna*
Mr Malausenna
☎ *93.79.70.06*

Madone de Fenestre
⌂ *CAF*

ACCOMMODATION GUIDE

See CAF Nice for information

Madone d'Utelle
06450 Lantosque
⌂ *Agapé*

Menton
06500 Menton
⌂ *Auberge les Santons*
Mr Busby
☎ *93.35.94.10*
⌂ *De Londres*
Mr Bensoussan
☎ *93.35.74.62*
⌂ *Le Globe*
Mr Pelletier
☎ *93.35.73.03*
⌂ *New-York*
Mr Mena
☎ *93.35.78.69*

Méolans-Revel
04340 Méolans
⌂
Monique Boek-Holt
☎ *92.81.26.27*

Refuge de Merveilles
⌂ *CAF*
See CAF Nice for information

La Pare
04400 Barcelonette
⌂ *ONF*
☎ *92.81.00.32*

Les Pras
04530 Sainte-Anne-le-Condamine
⌂ *Belvedere*
☎ *92.84.30.16*

Nice
06000 Nice
⌂ *Le Relais de Rimiez*
Mme Petruschi
☎ *93.81.18.65*
⌂ *Les Gemeaux*
Mr Dieude
☎ *93.89.03.60*
☎ *93.26.90.38*
⌂ *CAF Refuge de Nice*

See CAF Nice for information

Roure
06420 Saint-Sauveur-sur-Tinée
⌂ *Le Robur*
☎ *93.02.03.57*
⌂ *Vacherie de Roure*
☎ *93.02.00.70*
☎ *93.02.00.37*

Roya
⌂
J Murris
☎ *93.02.41.46*

Saint-Dalmas-Valdeblore
06420 Saint-Sauveur-sur-Tinée
⌂ *GTA*
☎ *93.02.83.96*

Saint-Etienne-de-Tinée
06660 Saint-Etienne-de-Tinée
⌂ *Des Amis*
Mr Fulconis
☎ *93.02.40.30*

Saint-Martin-Vésubie
06450 Saint-Martin-Vésubie
⌂ *Le Touron*
☎ *93.03.21.32*
⌂ *Les Champouns*
☎ *93.03.23.72*

Saint-Paul-sur-Ubaye
⌂
Mr Colin
☎ *92.84.32.99*

Saint -Sauveur-sur-Tinée
06420 Mairie de Saint-Sauveur-sur-Tinée
⌂
☎ *93.02.00.22*

Seignas Col de Clapouse
⌂
Information from the ADRI
☎ *92.31.07.01*

Sélonnet
04460 Sélonnet
⌂ *De Surville*

Mr Stordeur
☎ *92.35.00.81*

Sisteron
04200 Sisteron
Centre Aéré de Chantereine
☎ *92.61.00.37*

Sorine
Information from the ADRI
☎ *92.31.07.01*

Sospel
06380 Sospel
⌂ *De France*
Mr Volle
☎ *93.14.00.01*
⌂ *l'Auberge Provencal*
Mme Luciano
☎ *93.04.00.31*
⌂ *Des Etrangers*
Mr Domerego
☎ *93.04.00.09*

Tende
06430 Tende
⌂ *Miramonti*
Mr Maubert
☎ *93.04.61.82*
⌂ *Les Carlines*
☎ *93.04.62.74*

Turini (Col de)
06440 l'Escarene
⌂ *Le Ranch*
Mr Lupi
☎ *93.91.57.23*
⌂ *Les Chamois*
Mr Martos
☎ *93.91.57.42*
⌂ *Les Trois Vallées*
Mr l'Hommede
☎ *93.91.57.21*
⌂ *Le Logis*
☎ *93.91.58.18*

Utelle
06450 Lantosque
⌂ *Bellevue*
Mr Martinon
☎ *93.03.17.19*

INDEX

Details of bus/train connections have been provided wherever it was possible. We suggest you refer also to the map inside the front cover.